Common
Table

Common Table

An uncommon tale of
friendship and food

Janice Marriott   Virginia Pawsey

HarperCollins*Publishers*

Céad míle fáilte an chlann, Mia — Janice
To Harry, with love — Virginia

HarperCollins*Publishers*

First published 2010
HarperCollins*Publishers (New Zealand) Limited*
P.O. Box 1, Auckland 1140

HarperCollins*Publishers*

31 View Road, Glenfield, Auckland 0627, New Zealand
25 Ryde Road, Pymble, Sydney, NSW 2073, Australia
A 53, Sector 57, Noida, UP, India
77–85 Fulham Palace Road, London W6 8JB, United Kingdom
2 Bloor Street East, 20th floor, Toronto, Ontario M4W 1A8, Canada
10 East 53rd Street, New York, NY 10022, USA

National Library of New Zealand Cataloguing-in-Publication Data

Marriott, Janice.
Common table / Janice Marriott, Virginia Pawsey.
ISBN 978-1-86950-841-8
1. Marriott, Janice—Correspondence. 2. Pawsey, Virginia—
Correspondence. 3. Women cooks—New Zealand—
Correspondence. 4. Cooks—New Zealand—Correspondence.
I. Pawsey, Virginia. II. Title.
641.5092293—dc 22

Cover design by Priscilla Nielsen
Cover image by shutterstock.com
Internal illustrations by Pauline Whimp
Typesetting by IslandBridge

Printed by Griffin Press, Australia
70gsm Classic used by HarperCollins*Publishers* is a natural, recyclable
product made from wood grown in sustainable forests. The
manufacturing processes conform to the environmental regulations
in the country of origin, Finland.

Janice's Introduction

My standing-room-only kitchen in my small inner-city cottage is like a kitchen on a yacht. There are cupboards and drawers on two parallel sides. The third side, separating these two, is the width of the oven. A bright-blue bench runs around the three sides. I love putting gifts from the garden — lemons, tomatoes, feijoas, nasturtiums or poppies — on the blue bench. The wall opposite the oven holds a skinny fridge and some pull-out shelves. The sink is under the kitchen window which looks out over the garden. I depend on my garden the way most people depend on the produce section of their supermarket, or you farmers depend on your sheep. OK, so there's a supermarket 5 minutes walk away. But you never know when the motorway overbridge might fall down. Always best to be prepared. My garden could be regarded as my earthquake-preparedness kit. Maybe I've been an office worker too long . . .

My kitchen is so small that Bunsen the old Labrador couldn't lie down in it. While I cooked he used to lie in the doorway, monitoring the progress. He was the official taster, and his reaction always gave me an inflated idea of my culinary prowess.

I don't have too much time or space here for complicated chemical reactions, but I love to cook so I have a few rules. I cook simply and I clean up as I cook. I never have benches full of dishes to clean after cooking a meal. I eat ordinary food that hasn't come into the house in boxes, packets, tins, jars or on its own legs. But I do have some exceptions. I buy anchovies, sardines and mackerel in tins. I buy tins of chickpeas. A quick mash with coriander, chilli and garlic and you have a Friday evening dip — the most essential food item on my social calendar. I buy tinned tomatoes in the winter. Cooked down a bit, with a bit of garlic sautéed with whatever garden herbs are still providing leaves, they make great tomato sauce. Cooked down a bit more, and they coat a pizza.

I like New Zealand food: grass-fed happy beef, pumpkin soup, and seafood poached in coconut cream. I buy 'good' bread, which is now called 'artisan' bread. I use butter, not margarine. I use lots of olive oil, but most food, including omelettes and mushrooms, taste better in butter. I don't buy frozen pastry. I like making pastry, and what is a kitchen without flour in it? I love making scones.

A quick meal starts with me in the garden hunting for whatever's thriving. It might end up in a pasta sauce or in an omelette with fried sage leaves crumbled over it. In winter I might fill a casserole or a roasting dish and put it in the oven for a couple of hours. I love the smell of cooking in the house. I like to watch Tenz the cat sitting staring at the oven door, swaying slightly. A little black pottle of Kapiti ice cream is the perfect dessert with stewed fruit from the garden.

It's been a big year for me, making big decisions about my life. I can't worry and do the pros and cons lists without resorting to my favourite junk foods, which are peanuts, licorice and chocolate.

Virginia's Introduction

A big box-window in my kitchen captures the early morning sun. In the summertime it lights the white walls and warms the round oak table in the middle of the room; from the window I can see the kitchen garden, overblown with vegetables, the roses are in full bloom and I cannot wait to go out into the day. In the wintertime the sun is thin and frail and the garden hibernates, white and frozen or drab and brown under a grey winter sky. On winter mornings I huddle in the kitchen, hugging the speckled green coal range and do not want to leave its comforting, beating warmth.

A farm house kitchen is the heart and soul of the house. It is not just the room where food is cooked, it is the room where everything happens: it's where plans and budgets are discussed, it's where casual visitors sit for a cup of tea, where the bank manager lays out the loan forms to be signed, it's where births are celebrated and deaths are wept over, it's where we talk about our hopes and dreams, it's where we eat most of our meals. At the very heart of the kitchen, an old oak table stands encircled by six oak chairs with padded leather seats and that is where we sit. The wall opposite the window is taken up with a huge bookcase which is full of recipe books, reference books, poetry books, and rows of rustic pottery casserole dishes and jugs. The rest of the kitchen is lined with floor-to-ceiling rimu cupboards and bins for flour and sugar, and then there is the speckled green coal range which, whilst not an aesthetic asset, is very dearly loved. There are days when the snow snaps the power lines and the old coal range smokes on, warming the house, heating the water and cooking the meals, and I wonder how I would ever do without her.

A wide stainless-steel bench lies under the box-window, and that is where I work. Beneath the bench there is a big stainless-steel oven, a Titan, which has the great good fortune to be able to clean itself; above the oven sits an induction cook-top which is finger-tip sensitive and very fast on impatient days, and very slow for things that take time like pickles and jams. I am a farm-house cook, cursed or blessed, I'm not sure which, with the need to be able to make everything. I know it would be much simpler to go out and buy bread and buns, chocolates and ice cream, pasta and pastry, chicken stock and pesto, and I do if I don't have time; but when I do have time I enjoy spending hours in the kitchen mucking about with food.

March

Dear Virginia

My friend Jane said, on our Sunday afternoon walk, that it was a walk like 'we used to do'. I'm not sure what she meant by that because of course it wasn't anything like any of our regular Sunday walks for the last thirteen years. On that yellow beach at Island Bay no Bunsen panted along beside us. Bunsen was dead, and the picnic — we always have a picnic on the Sunday walk — lacked that wonderful quality of performance; us performing for a rapt audience of one concentrating, drooling dog.

We met a yellow Lab lunging through the shallows then spindling himself onto the sand, turning, using his ear as his leading edge: whack! His wet body, thick as a dolphin, hit the sand and he rolled back and forth, happy as a sand Lab, which he was. That was lovely.

Ah well. Let's just walk on.

When I walk, I think. I know you think on your hills, too. What will this year hold? No. I must reword this. I can't have spent all my life working in a bureaucracy, being force-fed all those assertiveness and team-building and communication workshops, and not learnt how to be 'proactive' and positive and in control. What I meant to ponder was: What will I make happen this year? (Time has sped up so much for me now that when I get around to making New Year Resolutions it is already March.) I think that maybe I want to learn to live without a salary. I can feel a fight developing between the me who I have become, and the me of my upbringing. In this corner is the working-class girl from the immigrant family for whom having a job and working hard was the goal, and there, in that corner, is the woman who wants less of the office hierarchy, more honesty in her life, and fewer dealings with people who can't think straight because of the language they abuse. I enjoy my work and admire my colleagues' skills and their dedication, but I don't want, any more, to get to work in the morning and find an email in office-speak saying: 'We acknowledge that a small number of you may have only recently captured your deliverables as formal objectives . . .' It used to be funny. Now it's tragic.

But, hey, while I wallow in regret for time lost, I will keep that picture of the drooling Bunsen in the forefront of my mind. He knew what was important in life. So, following his example, I will think a lot this year about food.

PS: Can you send me that courgette recipe you told me about last year? I've got too many courgettes.

Hello, Janice

As you fight your bureaucracy you will love this story of bureaucratic excess in Canterbury. Contact Energy is replacing the power poles up the road; this means the power will be off for six days between 9am and 4pm for us and it will be off for much longer for farms further up the road. We have three electricity meters on the farm, so we always receive three communications about anything that Contact does. Because the power is out for six days and we received an advisory letter for each day it is out — times three — we received eighteen letters about the repair work. Mandy and Dugald received twenty letters, and we worked out that Malcom at the end of the road must have received about forty.

Enough of silly bureaucracy; I want to talk about my culinary inheritance. I received my first formal cooking lessons at 'manual'. Manutuke school pupils in Standards Five and Six were bussed into Central School in Gisborne once a week to attend cooking and woodwork classes; cooking was for girls and woodwork was for boys. The cooking tutor was Mrs Lincoln. There was a thrilling rumour whispered about that Mrs Lincoln was a shearing cook and not a proper teacher at all. Whatever the truth, she was a gifted teacher and a good sensible cook. I remember how much I looked forward to cooking days as I set off with my little enamel billy and pie dish and my white apron and cap with *Virginia* embroidered on the front in red cotton.

My mother was a fervent reader of books about food. From her I learnt to be adventurous. We were reputed to eat weird food at our house: fried cabbage, duck livers, artichokes and strange green-skinned pears that weren't pears at all. Whenever we visited Wellington there was a pilgrimage to the Dixon Street deli where we stocked up on salami and smelly cheeses and olives and real coffee. Mother enjoyed hosting dinner parties, but they were what I call academic dinner parties. For her, food was the main event. The guests were necessary incidentals — though they did have to be deipnosophists for the evening to be declared a success.

Dear Virginia

That word is not in my dictionary.

When I was a child my parents had a guesthouse and my nana cooked. All day long the kitchen had food in interesting stages of preparation. Meat slow-cooking in the oven. Pastry being rolled out on the marble slab. Fruit in bowls to be picked over, peeled, then sliced. Even though we were a large family, I had my fair share of turns at cleaning out the bowl after the cakes had been mixed. I was allowed to use a fork to prick my J into the tops of pastries or pies, allowed to stir sauces and set table. Shopping for, preparing, cooking, eating and cleaning up after our meals took up most of the time the family was together, and not at work or school.

Now I do meal-planning after work as I walk my empty stomach home along The Terrace. I always cook from scratch. I never buy pre-cooked soups and mixes, or meals' in tins or compartmentalized trays. Part of eating, for me, is the preparation. Even when I'm alone at home, and I often am, I make an evening meal. The moving around the kitchen, opening drawers and cupboards, finding the right knife or grater, making something, is my way of being at home in the evening, using my home. If I just opened a plastic bubble of supermarket soup and ate that I'd feel unsatisfied. Maybe some of it is that 'make my hands busy to keep the world at bay' thing, but not all of it. I enjoy cooking the way I like gardening; I like getting my hands dirty.

Walking home today it was hard to think about dinner. I kept thinking about our new phones. We'd had a team lesson in programming our new phones. I noticed the guys all set their ring tones lower than the girls. Tina had to blow into her phone as a 'connectedness' test. Someone asked if it was her first obscene phone call and what it felt like. Sarah puts vanilla oil on the receiver to remove any germs and keep it sweet-smelling.

PS: Loved the Contact Energy story!

Dear Janice

I mull over thoughts as I knead the weekly bread. This is what I think about your battle with office bureaucracy: become a consultant. Consultants are people who resign and then hire themselves out to their former employer for at least four times the hourly rate they were being paid before they resigned, and everybody is happy.

People quail at the thought of bread baking, but it is not difficult; yeast is a wonderfully forgiving baking agent. The only thing you can do to offend yeast is heat it too much when you dissolve it in water right at the beginning of the procedure; it can be killed. Yeast bakers will of course say you have to be seriously precise about temperature and density and so on, but I find that you can make many breads without the exact precision they speak of. After all, the peasants who made what we call 'ethnic breads' didn't have thermometers and fancy yeasts and the fine-ground flours we use today.

You wanted my courgette recipe. This is one for the more mature courgette, the one you let get away for a few days. It is not a marrow, you understand, just an over-large courgette, about the size of a small cucumber.

The Courgette That Got Away

Slice into thick slices and fry in a little hot olive oil until browned. At the same time heat a jar of tomato mix, whichever flavour you fancy; of course if you grow your own tomatoes you could make your own savoury tomato mix.

Transfer the slices of courgette to a flat dish and pour the tomato sauce around them so they look like little islands in a thick red sea. Top the islands with grated Tasty cheese, chopped fresh oregano and black pepper, then pop under the grill until the cheese is bubbly and slightly browned. This dish looks smart and the courgettes are transformed from boring and squishy to firm and delicious.

Deipnosophist — I love it, a word you do not know! A deipnosophist is a person skilled in dining and table talk. My new *Oxford Dictionary*, the tenth edition, appears to have dropped the word, which is a pity.

Now I have to go out and shift the wether lambs onto the rape. The sun is shining.

Dear Virginia

I took Friday off work — such a rare decision for me — and left the office behind and headed up Highway One. I arrived at Bill's, out of Raurimu, in time for an early dinner and the now-famous cream sponge — recipe in *Common Ground*. We stared up at hawks on the 200-feet-high, ninety-year-old Norwegian spruce. I watched the thistledown blowing — just the way Denis Glover described it in 'Sings Harry'. Tui belched at each other.

Kereru thrashed about in the hoheria tree. No programmable phones. Great. Then we drove on, 40 ks, to Taumarunui to surprise the members of the Taumarunui Writers' Group at their Friday night meeting. Out the side window, Taranaki, at sunset, was like a giant pyramid in a flaming red desert.

The meeting was in ex-Taumarunui-librarian Helen's huge sitting room: comfortable sofas, flokati rugs, giant coffee tables, the clatter of platters, cheese, crackers, bottles of wine. The group's a perfect way to relax for a couple of hours, share the joys and frustrations of writing, get other people to listen to your as-yet-unpublished words.

When we walked in, Margee was saying to Glenda, 'We want to know what happens next', about her story that she'd circulated to them all via email. Glenda said she'd like to know as well. Any suggestions? Everyone laughed. Margee, South African, is a physics teacher at the high school. She paints watercolours, and has 40 acres of blueberries. I was interested in the blueberries more than the story. I was sorry not to see Dorothy the black Zimbabwean ex-hospital-matron, but she's got a better job in Hamilton now. Bill told me about the time he drove to the blueberry farm and saw Dorothy walking down a row with a basket of blueberries balanced on her head.

I bought blueberries the next day. The two pickers, who pick and process as they go, and do 10 kilos in a day easily, are seventy-one and seventy-seven years old. 'Picked 3 tonnes this year,' one said. 65% of the crop is picked by p.y.o. tourists — $5 an ice-cream-container full. Margee explained that blueberries sweat a lot. When I got them home, she said, I had to spread them out and pat them dry before storing them in the fridge without covering them.

Across the road from the farm, in Owhango, is a stylish café, Out of the Fog. It's the best café on Highway 4 (if you exclude

Clowns in Raetihi). Margee told me she goes to the Fog for breakfast most days. Some dairy farmers go there for a coffee after milking. Tourists go for early breakfasts before biking round the mountains or setting off for the Grand Traverse. We said hi to Jonathan, who lives in Margee's house and helps out in the Fog. He was just back from a 2½-hour barista course in Auckland to learn how to make the coffee.

The perfect thing to do with blueberries after a long car journey is to make smoothies for the kids.

Smoothies
We just whizz up equal amounts of blueberries, strawberries, green tea and yoghurt. Add sugar or honey to taste.

Good morning, Janice

We have a stylish café, too. It's called The Rocking Frog; only a 16k drive to the nearest capuccino — would you survive?

As I was kneading my Good Friday hot cross buns at my kitchen bench, dreaming, with my hands working the soft brown dough, I looked out over the lawn, a delphinium grove, the lush green grass of the orchard, to Kit's stone in the shadow of the eucalyptus trees, the memorial stone with the bronze plaque that catches the morning sunlight. The plaque commemorates the lives of Kit and his friends who died at Cave Creek. It reads:

KIT PAWSEY 25.8.77 – 28.4.95
AT CAVE CREEK, PUNAKAIKI

THE CAVE CREEK TRAGEDY. A VIEWING PLATFORM COLLAPSED AT CAVE CREEK SOUTH ON THE 28TH APRIL 1995 KILLING THIRTEEN STUDENTS AND ONE CONSERVATION OFFICER.

I thought about Easter and the way it was. Kneading dough is a soporific, nostalgic, comforting indulgence. Everyone should knead dough; it is therapeutic. Because both hands are immersed in dough which is sticky to begin with and becomes more elastic and less clingy as it is worked, you cannot use your hands for anything else. There is no opportunity for multi-tasking and so you sink into gentle reverie.

Easter at Double Tops was always a celebratory weekend — not, I have to admit, a celebration of Christ and the resurrection, but a celebration of life and family and food. On Friday, I made hot cross buns. On Saturday, the house and shearers' quarters filled with guests for the Easter Saturday dinner and the Great Easter Egg Hunt on Sunday morning.

I always cooked lamb for the Saturday dinner. An Easter lamb is a tasty beast. It is an older animal than the Christmas lamb, and it lends itself well to roasting with rosemary and garlic. Because I was always cooking for a great multitude, I cooked the well-roasted version. There is nothing more nightmarish than cooking meat the rare and rested way when you have guests who are difficult to move to the table at exactly the right moment for the meat.

Autumn is the time for roasted mixed vegetables, pumpkin, kumara, carrot, beetroot, roasted in olive oil and dressed with balsamic vinegar. If the frosts stay away there are fresh green beans and courgettes, late peas and tomatoes and corn. It is a sumptuous feasting time.

I cannot say that there was a traditional Easter dessert, but

I can say it was a creation that had to be carried to the table on a wide, round platter. Harry's favourite was a chocolate rum charlotte. Mine was anything made with meringue, a meringue basket filled with fruit and cream, Gateau Diane, or just a good New Zealand pavlova. I am not good at making soft, mile-high marshmallow pavlovas, so it would have been a crunchy pavlova. After dessert there was coffee and chocolates and port and cigars. Many people smoked in those days. The dining table would be littered with full ashtrays by the end of the evening. Guests smoked between courses. No one had heard of second-hand smoke. How times have changed. Smokers, if there are any now, puff furtively out in the cold night air. I always kept cigars in the dining-room dresser for after-dinner smoking. Port and cigars led to 'solving the problems of the world' discussions which would last a long way into the morning because no one had to drive home, or if they did it was only to a neighbouring farm on the Virginia Road.

Next morning I became the Easter Bunny. I departed from the living room where the children sat with curtains drawn — so no one could see where the Easter Bunny hid the eggs — laden with baskets of bright foil-covered Easter eggs. As the children grew older the Easter Bunny roamed more widely, dropping eggs in the clefts of trees, the tops of fence posts, the hen house and stables, the shrubberies and in the flower beds. The children never found all the eggs and I could never remember where I had hidden every single one, so for months afterwards I would discover Easter eggs as I gardened.

The year Kit died we held what all the children (our two and their cousins) decided would be 'The Last Great Easter Egg Hunt'. Kirstie was nineteen, Kit and Jennie seventeen, Fleur was fifteen and Clair was twelve, and they all knew that childhood could not last forever. After the hunt my friend Jenny photographed the hunters with their booty. They are standing under the weeping elm. The leaves of the tree are turning and the lawn is sprinkled with golden leaves. The children are smiling; each clutches a bag of eggs in one hand, and with the other they hold an egg between thumb and forefinger. It is a happy photo, the record of The Last Great Easter Egg Hunt.

The phone rang just as I finished kneading the buns and putting away my dreams. It was Terry (the Terryfier) ringing from Honiara where he has been on a peace-keeping mission with the New Zealand Army. He has rung several times during his tour of duty. Peace-keeping in the Solomons sounds tedious, hot and very sticky. Terry told me that religion is 'big in the Solomons', the churches are always full on Sundays and 'they will be full this Easter', he said, 'but I won't be there,' he added with great glee. He is coming home on Easter Sunday, and he's very much looking forward to resuming civilian life. He wanted to know if I was writing another book. In his experience everyone wants to write about him. He was employed as a fencer for a few months over one summer at Castle Hill when Christine Ferneyhough was writing her book *The Road to Castle Hill*. He stayed in the shearers' quarters, which are considerably more upmarket than the Double Tops quarters. '$400 sheets,' he told me.

The buns are cooked now. I have taken a photograph to send to you. They are golden brown and glistening with a sticky glaze, and Harry and I have eaten two each for lunch, dripping with butter and still warm from the oven. This afternoon I am taking Val and her children from the cottage, up the road to Haydon Downs where we are going to pick nectarines. I shall give some of the hot cross buns to Val and some to Heather and Barry in exchange for the fruit. There are no Easter visitors at

Double Tops to eat hot cross buns any more, but I still enjoy making them and giving them away.

Hot Cross Buns

These buns are soft and dense and spicy and yummy.

1¼ cups warmed milk
1 tbsp brown sugar
4 tsp Surebake yeast
75g butter
1 egg, beaten
½ cup brown sugar
4 cups best flour
1 tbsp cinnamon
2 tbsp mixed spice
½ tsp salt
1 tbsp dark cocoa
1 cup mixed sultanas and currants

Warm the milk (to comfortable bath heat) and add 1 tbsp brown sugar. Sprinkle the Surebake onto the mixture, wait 5 minutes then add 1 cup of flour. Mix thoroughly, cover with cling-film and leave for half an hour.

Cream the butter and sugar and add the beaten egg, mix into the dough mixture then add the spices, salt, cocoa and the dried fruit, then slowly add 2 cups of the flour. Stir with a wooden spoon until the mixture is firm.

Tip the dough onto a floured bench and then gradually add the rest of the flour. I say gradually add the remaining flour as each yeast dough mix is slightly different depending on the flour, the size of the egg and your mood. If you add all the flour at once and it is too much, the dough will be dry

and hard and it is very difficult to remedy a dry dough mix —
you will end with dry hard buns.

Knead the dough on the bench until it is shiny and
silky smooth and doesn't stick to your hands any more —
about 10 minutes — and dream or listen to music, or both.

Return the dough to the bowl, cover with film or a wet
tea towel and leave it for an hour. After an hour, take the
dough and place it on a board, cut into 16 equal portions
and shape into buns, put buns into a baking dish with sides
or a meat dish which will confine the buns into a batch.
Make crosses with short pastry. Leave the buns to rise until
double in size.

Bake in a hot oven 200 degrees for 12–15 minutes. Glaze
with syrup as soon as they are removed from the oven. To
make the glaze, dissolve 2 tsp of golden syrup in 2 tbsp hot
water and bring to the boil.

Tomorrow I will be driving out to Tommy's Cabin with the lawn
mower, to mow the croquet lawns for an Easter Monday meet
of the Tommy's Cabin Croquet Club. The theme this Easter
is The British Raj. We meet at 11. Tiffin is at one. We will eat
kedgeree and chapattis and curry and dhal and poppadums
and other Indian fare. Happy Easter!

Dear Virginia

The photos of the baking rack full of perfect shiny buns almost
made me drool like a Labrador. What effort! What achievement.
I must tell you a story about food photos. Margaret, a workmate,

sometimes has foreign-language students to stay. She cooks for them. At present she has a Japanese woman staying who photographs every plate of food Margaret cooks for her and then puts the photos up on her student blog.

My Easter is very different. Easter for me isn't roast lamb. It's salads. It isn't slow cooking in a coal range. It's more assembling deli food and garden vegetables. It's easy, lazy entertaining. We had a family lunch and tried to include people who were far away, in America and England. This meant the laptop was shaded with a cardboard hat while we ate outside under the rose pergola, waiting for the *boing* that signalled someone was there ready to speak to us. When the call came we showed them the food laid out on the table — the meats, the salads — Greek, green, bean, tomato and basil. I walked around the garden with the laptop facing outward so they could see what was blooming and what was being eaten by bugs. I turned the laptop around and saw my brother-in-law's feet walking up his stairs. As I watched the screen, I started climbing the virtual stairs. Result: I nearly fell into Graham Thomas, the yellow rose bush.

The most popular salad was lettuce, rocket, chives, coriander with grated radishes, and a creamy lemon dressing. It was served inside a huge curled Iceberg lettuce leaf — also from the garden. The second most popular was beetroot and apple.

And if you still have obese courgettes, here's a trick to play on them.

Ribboned Courgette Salad

Turn one around, longways. Use a wide potato peeler to slice very thin ribbons of courgette (with the skin on). Pile it up. Douse it with vinaigrette and plenty of lemon zest. It looks great and tastes good.

PS: A zester is my favourite kitchen utensil. I'm not keen on electrical appliances because my kitchen is so small. I don't like the bench space or storage space they take up. But a tiny lemon zester, the size of a potato peeler — it can brighten up so many meals.

Dear Janice

I don't like a lot of appliances either, but I do have a Kenwood mixer, now forty years old, still beating with a strong heart, and a food processor. My absolute favourite cooking utensil is an old-fashioned hand-held egg-beater. One of those solid ones everyone had in the 'fifties and 'sixties. It has wooden handles and big whisking balloons which can whip cream and beat eggs in nanoseconds. If you want to buy one you have to scout second-hand shops.

I discovered a beautiful and hardly-used egg-beater in the bottom drawer of a motel kitchen last year. I offered to buy it, but the motelier didn't know how much it was worth so he said, 'You buy me a new egg-beater and I will swap it with the old one.' I rushed to Briscoes and bought a useless new egg-beater and we swapped. My other favourites are a garlic-crusher with an olive-stoner in the handle, which used to belong to an English hostess, Margaret Lady Howell, my cast-iron frying pan and my old American waffle iron.

On Saturday we drove into the Lewis Pass to meet Fleur after her running race on the St James Walkway. She won the women's race in 8 hours and 5 minutes. The St James is normally a three- to four-day tramp of 70 ks. Fleur won $1,000 at the funniest prize-giving, where people had to do silly things to win spot prizes. Most of the contestants were limping. Some were wounded. Some were still running on in the dark and the pouring rain.

After the race we drove to Maruia Springs to soak in the hot rock pools and swat the man-eating sandflies. We love Maruia Springs, and the hotel which has always been a Basil Fawlty hostelry. Maruia Springs is a 'must stop' if you are ever driving over the Lewis Pass. It is owned by Japanese now and you imagine Japanese efficiency would prevail, but no. We were looking forward to a glass of wine, or a cold beer maybe, but at the front door we were greeted with this notice: *Due to administration error in application for liquor licence alcohol cannot be sold or consumed on the premises except in guest bedroom.* Fleur doesn't like wine so she was not bothered by the administrative error, but she did fancy an ice cream. There was a notice stuck to the wall above the freezer, it read: *Ice Cream 30% off. Ice cream melted once due to freezer malfunction, still great taste, just ugly shape.* We ordered coffee.

Dear Virginia

On a perfect blue day, while you were dagging, crutching or drafting, a group of us went picnicking on Somes Island.

The ferry looked as festive as a bowl of flowers, because of scores of people sprouting from the top of it, ogling the ever-changing views of Wellington. At the Somes wharf we were mustered into a whare kiore (that is what they call it) by eager DOC staff. We all had to take everything out of our day-packs and feel around inside them just in case we had a rat in our bag. The Japanese tourists were mystified. I was, too. Who would own up if they found one?

I pulled a *pan bagnat* out of my bag — it could easily have been a bomb, so well-wrapped was it and so carefully did I lay it down. Then I pulled out a long oven mitt, the sort with gloves on each end. Wrapped in this were four sharp knives, one a large bread knife.

The Japanese tourists were horrified. My Japanese wasn't quite good enough to explain to them that our border security isn't at all fazed by bombs or knives, just rats.

Rat-less, we were allowed out of the whare kiore and found a perfect picnic table, where we could sit in a secluded, shaded area off the track, at the top of a cliff. Wellington draped itself before us, across that sparkling water. We spread a linen cloth, opened our sparkling wine, and I ceremonially sliced the *pan bagnat*. We finished the meal with cake and chocolate from Moore Wilson, then lugged our now heavier bodies and lighter packs to the top of the island.

On top we were impressed by the gun emplacements that used to have giant guns pointing straight out between the heads into Cook Strait, waiting to take pot shots at the Japanese — warriors not tourists. After the war the guns were sold to the Japanese, who now come to see the locals engaging in strange rituals involving carrying sharp knives and possibly bombs up to where the guns used to be.

A *pan bagnat* is the perfect picnic when you have to carry the food for some distance in a backpack, without a chilly bin. When it's wrapped the way I wrap it, it is indestructible. The recipe is suitable for busy bureaucrats, and project managers who don't cook so much as assemble food. Here's the recipe.

Pan Bagnat

On Friday evening, at the supermarket, buy one big sourdough loaf. Buy tomatoes, garlic and lettuce in the veg section. (I used tomatoes and rocket from the garden.) Buy supresso from the deli counter. Get it sliced very thinly and longways rather than around the top, or get other salamis, or ham off the bone.

Buy olives from the same deli counter — fresh plump, juicy ones with no stones, stuffed green ones and black kalamatas. Buy some mild cheese — mozzarella is good. Find cold-pressed boutique olive oil.

At home drop all the bags — not plastic ones, I hope — on the kitchen floor. Change out of the suit and heels and tights. Open a wine and sit down. I can just get the last rays of the sun before it goes behind Tinakori Hill at this time of year. Open the mail — *sip* — IRD letter — *sip sip* — phone bill — *sip sip sip*. Then, refreshed, go to the assembly point, the kitchen bench. Put the loaf on your far left. (I'm left-handed so maybe you will have to reverse the instructions.) Then, in order, a large bread board, a pastry brush, a cheese mandolin, a tomato knife, the olive oil, garlic and crusher. Pile all those plastic-wrapped deli packets on the rest of the bench.

Saw the sourdough loaf horizontally. Gouge out some of the bread so you have before you what look like two waka. Crush garlic into a half-cup of olive oil, and brush it over the cut sides of the loaf. Then fill the base of the bread, layering up the chopped olives, the meats, sliced tomato, cheese, rocket or lettuce (not too much). Keep layering until it's nicely mounded, then put the top of the bread back on, making sure you have it around the right way so it's an exact fit.

Within the assembly structure there is room for creativity. Remember your last staff training day. What sort of person are you: an eagle, dove, turkey or dodo? Make your *pan bagnat* suit you and your team. If you want tuna instead of ham — use tuna. If you want it wetter, use more tomatoes. Make it your own. If in doubt, have a meeting about it with other interested parties.

And remember: dispute resolution is available in the form of the bottle of wine.

Glad-wrap your *pan bagnat* tightly. Put it in the fridge with a weight on top. I use a cast-iron casserole. Next day, picnic day, still glad-wrapped, put lots of elastic bands around it. Put it in another bag and put it in your pack. Don't forget the bread knife. I've read somewhere — but maybe I read too much — that Italian peasants used to make these and sit on them on the bus on the way to their picnic. (Was this before glad-wrap, I wonder?)

Hello, Janice

I hate one-up-manship, it is the root of rampant consumerism, but I cannot resist contesting your sandwich making. I'm sure I cannot trump a *pan bagnat* on Somes Island, but have you heard of the Double Tops Squashed Sandwich? After all, what is a *pan bagnat* but a squashed sandwich masquerading as a mysterious, sophisticated European picnic delicacy? We are not pretentious out in the hills back of Hawarden. We call a sandwich a sandwich. Last Wednesday we went 'out the back' to a Federated Farmers day at the Lakes Station. The Lakes is a 30,000-acre sheep and cattle station with Lakes Shepherd, Mason, Taylor and Sumner sitting within the boundaries. The Hurunui River flows through Lake Sumner.

I had to get up early in the morning to make a picnic lunch for the day out the back. I decided to make a sandwich much like yours, but as we do not have any delis down the road I had to raid the deep-freeze, the pantry, the fridge and the garden.

Double Tops Squashed Sandwich

From the deep-freeze I took a Double Tops Bakery *ciabatta*, I cut it in half and painted the bottom half with home-made mustard mayonnaise, then I layered rocket from the garden followed by garlic salami, tomatoes, Edam cheese from the fridge, a few olives, and then the lid, buttered.

I squashed the big sandwich flat, then I cut it into slices — we don't do naff things like carry a collection of kitchen knives when we go picnicking in the high country — and I bound each thick slice very tightly in glad-wrap. I squashed all the tight-bound sandwiches together in a container and popped it in a Susie's canvas picnic bag.

(Absolutely everyone should have a Susie's picnic bag. I'm not sure what we did before we bought ours.) Along with the squashed sandwich I took almond pound cake, apples from our apple tree, and a thermos of black tea.

We travelled many miles up the Hurunui River to eat our lunch in the shade of tall thick-trunked red beech trees. Beech trees shed their leaves all day in fine drifts like falling rain. They are beautiful. It was cool under the trees, so Harry and I found a log in the sunshine where I unwrapped the squashed sandwich. After lunch, we wandered in the beech forest evading the Federated Farmers annual general meeting.

Under the trees I espied the Chief Justice. See, it is not only on the streets of Wellington that one encounters important people. A mutual friend had said I must make myself known to her if I saw her, so I did. We did not talk about weighty matters of justice, at which I have to say I would have been totally at a loss. We talked farming and whether the Lakes Station ewes would winter well. The Chief Justice knows a lot about farming. She could have been a farmer not the Chief Justice, except for the red fingernails. They screamed 'city woman'.

Dear Virginia

Re the red-finger-nailed Chief Justice: did you know that in her Wellington workplace, the Supreme Court, a Japanese composting system is operated, by the staff, for their lunch leftovers — *bokashi*, it's called. A roster reveals whose turn it is to take the 'product' home.

April

Hello, Janice

I have just got in from dipping 1,000 two-tooths. We began in the dim light of dawn, and by the time the sun shone brightly we were down to the last thirty sheep. The sheep running in the early light ran through the dip tunnel as if it wasn't there. With sun-up, the wind was blowing through the dip the wrong way and blowing dip spray out the front where it created arching rainbows in the sunshine. Every last sheep had to be manhandled through the dip. Harry was coated with a fine mist of Diazinon, very toxic. When I told him this was dangerous, he flung a whole bucketful of expletives at me and told me to back off. I hate dipping, it's dirty, smelly, sweaty and very unglamorous. I am so looking forward to my visit to Wellington for the book launch, and I'm particularly looking forward to the make-over for the magazine photo shoot.

PS: Harry has just come in for morning tea. Dare I suggest he wash all that toxin right out of his hair?

Dear Virginia

The only dipping I do, of produce from my own rolling acres, is dipping artichoke leaves, one by one, into mayonnaise, or *crème fraiche* and lemon juice. (Just add a fresh herb — whatever's needing a haircut in the garden.) I don't usually get to 1,000 leaves. Artichokes are what I call 'atmosphere food'. You have to have time to spend, slowly drawing each leaf through your teeth. It's for two people. No point eating it by yourself. It's hard for an office worker to justify the time. It doesn't look good on a timesheet: *Ate one artichoke. 1 hour.*

Your sort of dipping sounds gruelling and maybe even a Health and Safety issue for our HR team to write a report about. The poisonous chemical is a worry. We had a Health and Safety alert at work this week when a few fruit flies had been seen in one of the loos. An all-staff urgent email went round: *Tena koutou. Following feedback from staff the Fruit Fly spraying scheduled for tonight has been deferred. We would prefer to carry the spraying out over a long weekend or holiday break and need to work through the logistics of this with our provider. We will advise you when we have further information. Ka kite.*

I also fear contemplating what our Health and Safety people would do about Harry's swearing. Probably send you both off to a training workshop where you get to wear silly hats and find out whether you are an eagle or a dove. Swearing, as an employee or employer, would get you an Official Warning in the office. I'd love to let rip occasionally and hurl abuse at some idiot across the meeting-room table. But offices are about repression. You sit in front of a computer, under fluorescent lights, in a huge open-plan glare belt with no privacy, and no matter how furious you are you must never explode. How do people do it? They seek solace in cake and chocolate.

I took another day off work — I've discovered I like them — and arranged for a guy to clip my out-of-control hedges. He's a hunter and we talked about hunting. He likes to go out alone. It's not for sharing, he said. I told him that you could chop up — I wasn't sure whether 'butcher' was the right term — a cow. He was very impressed. Then John, an actor friend, arrived with his small helper (daughter Annamika). Bruce the hunter immediately said, 'Oh, that's Dutch isn't it?' and everyone got on like a house on fire. I brewed more coffee. John put up some Lundia shelves, then I had to dash off to a lunch with workmates on the waterfront in blistering heat — really — under umbrellas. Workers were lying on the seats by the water, their white shirts as startling as gulls' breasts against the blue sea.

Robert is at this moment holed up in a cheap hotel in Vancouver doing on-line exams on his laptop, hoping to pass and get a job helicoptering in the Arctic for the long daylight hours of the Northern summer. I was worried about him, so I went to a garden centre — an out-of-character event — and bought a columnar apple tree to replace the hapless lilac in the middle of the garden. Cost $50. Then I lost my car key. The day seemed to be turning bad. I arrived home to find Alison had left a huge jar of roasted walnuts on my verandah.

Good morning, Janice

Just off out to shift cattle and lambs. It takes a lot of organization to leave the farm for a day or two. We finished the dipping yesterday: as I said last time, quite the deadliest job on the farm. Flying chemicals, back-breaking, shoulder-wrenching. If anything is going to kill or maim us it will be the dipping. Harry and I shoved 2,000 mixed-age ewes through the dip on our own yesterday. The Terryfier had made himself very scarce, and Jason was away racing greyhounds. Every time the ewes stopped running it was my dogs' fault or my fault; it is the boss's prerogative to blame the underlings. Harry and I yelled at each other a lot, the ewes did not run well, there was muddy, shitty water in the race because of overnight rain, a horrible experience but we won't have to repeat the performance for another six months.

Dear Virginia

I am looking forward to seeing you in Wellington next week. I assure you there will be no shaggy ewes to dip. Just to make sure you aren't confused about this, I have had my hair cut in an attempt to differentiate me from an old ewe. I left the hairdresser's with $120 of 'product'. My hair now looks short and wild instead of longer and wild. And I am wild because I was talked into all this stupid 'product'. In fact I am so wild I might have to buy a bar of Whittaker's Dark, with Almonds.

At work today I was talking to a wan young project assistant, who looks as though she's seen as much sunlight this year as a giant squid. We discussed our techniques for getting through the day. She told me she gets through the morning by thinking about what she's going to buy for lunch. She said, 'I like my lunch to be a surprise to break up the big unsurprise of the day. Having Marmite-and-lettuce sandwiches waiting for me in the bottom of my bag does not give me something to look forward to after a morning of dull work.'

She's young, beautiful and newly married. I wanted to whisk her out of her computer 'pod' and tell her to go tailing or dipping or anything with a bit of energy and mayhem. Her favourite lunch, and pre-lunch dream about lunch — *tostadas* from the Mexican in the food court.

Hello, Janice

Thank you, thank you, thank you, for a totally off-the-farm experience. I arrived home intoxicated with the city, with cafés, book launches, restaurants, motorized towel dispensers, make-up artists, photo shoots, cappuccinos; it was all so seductive. I looked longingly from the tiny aeroplane window at the diminishing city as we flew away and wondered how I would cope with withdrawal. Yesterday in a state of high discontent I decided that a cold-turkey detox was the only way to go. I wheeled my mountain bike out of its shed and rode off into the hills. I rode to the gateway of the Double Tops block in the middle of the farm and I lay on the grass and looked up at the clear blue sky. There are thousands of insects dancing reels in the sky if you ever stop to look. Fantails chased the dancing insects, and in the beech tree bush the bellbirds chortled amongst themselves. I lay there for a long time and let the sun beat into my face as I tried to empty my mind of the city.

This morning my dogs and I brought the rising two-year-old steers in from the Back Plateau for TB testing. As I have said before, you cannot hurry a cow and nor can you rush a steer. If you rush steers they stampede and smash gates and fences. A mob of steers is like a busload of unruly schoolboys on a rugby tour, brainless when excited. So we ambled all the way in at a calm pace. On the radio the weekly debate from political left and political right was taking place, it was another tedious tit-for-tat about the Electoral Finance Act. I drifted off. Was it really only two days ago that you and I were lunching at Nikau café, with the Labour Party conference going on next door, I wondered? It seemed weeks ago that we had to leave two full and untouched cups of coffee cooling on the table and rush off to an interview, absolutely weeks ago; I knew then I was detoxified.

If you return from a sojourn in the country, do you have to undergo a reverse process and wind yourself up? Have to go. We are off out the back to Rollets to find some cows.

Dear Virginia

'You cannot hurry a cow.' That's what you said. That thinking wouldn't help me explain a blown-out timeline on a project for a major client. 'This is a project you just can't hurry,' I imagine saying at a meeting in a windowless room, while thinking of you mustering slow steers plodding uphill.

I've been in Auckland for a few days. Dogs are everywhere in Auckland. None of them has the refinement of Bunsen. Most of them take themselves for walks and, like human Aucklanders, their idea of a good time is to walk around the shops. There I was, buying some bananas and this hound comes up and widdles all over a box of cauli. I kicked it with my vintage Para Rubber Commandos and it bit me. I'm sure it couldn't have brought the rising two-year-old steers in from the Back Plateau. I had to have a massive coffee and cake in the Volcanic on Mt Eden Road to recover.

You don't see biddable dogs up there, like Labs or beardies. It's all Rotties the shape of mahogany coffee tables, or German shepherds looking for a decent feed and eyeing you up as a possible takeaway. However, I have found one place where women walk up and down with poodles, miniature collies and spaniels on leads. Puriri Drive in Cornwall Park. They're the sort of women who are grateful to their dogs for 'getting them out of the house'. At lunchtime tradesmen park there, let their pent-up dogs out for a bite of spaniel and a pint of widdle, then sit, in the ute, eating sammies and reading magazines.

The Auckland dinner was marred by Gerald's ordering live baby octopus. He poked them with his chopsticks and they tried to crawl out of the bowl. We left the restaurant and went to the Irish bar, The Bog, in Parnell. Everyone there is really Irish, really dancing, and really drunk. It's a great place to go if you want to drink all evening and not feel the need to move on. It also holds quiz nights. I often visit Auckland, and I've never been on a winning quiz night team but I have drunk more than normal in the attempt. Two nights ago we were swept out of there at 1am by a guy with a broom.

I spent last night out at Paekakariki Beach and this morning it was back to work. Yes, to answer your question, when I've been away I do go through the reverse process. I have to put aside all the tactile, sensuous things I enjoy — the sun, the smells of plants, the sea, and conversations and feasting — and turn into an office worker who has high expectations of no pleasures at all, except a reliable pay cheque.

This is what I did today: I joined the Long March along the Quays, in the dark, from the train station to the office, getting jostled the whole way like an apple on an inspection belt. I dodged buskers with guitar cases open on the pavement for me to fall into, women walking towards me, not looking where they were going, looking instead into their cleavage as they talked on their cellphones, their breasts swathed in cross-over cotton like an Egyptian mummy gone walkabout. I swerved out of the path of guys — lawyers, bureaucrats — thrusting forward with steel-cornered briefcases that could knee-cap me. I passed electricians on Lambton Quay, fixing the electrics in a McDonald's sign. I overtook workmen laying pavers and more pavers. (Lambton Quay is looking more like a sample walk in a garden centre than the fabled Golden Mile at the moment.) And all the while I was preparing myself. My shoes, heels; my skirt, straight and lined; my bag over one arm — all indicated control, constriction.

Then I turned in, through glass doors that magically slid open as I raised my bag with the swipe card tucked inside it. I was in the faux marble foyer. Outside the lifts were the plastic crates of milk cartons — yellow tops and just a couple of light blue. You always get yellow-top milk in government offices and publishing houses. It's the predominance of women on staff.

I left the dawn light behind and got into a silently pursing lift. I rubbed my bag over the number pad. My hidden swipe card recognized me as someone who belonged, and the lift door closed. I bowed my head. Everyone does, at 7am, in a lift with mirror walls. Soon the door to the office opened. Another day began.

I bathed in the cold blue rectangle of light in front of my computer screen. How come we settle for so little fun out of life? I thought of you, in the Canterbury hills, mustering on horseback, or making something clever with a hundred obese zucchini.

PS: Loved the Tommy's Cabin photos.

Hello, Janice

I am pleased you have at last seen the photos of the Tommy's Cabin Croquet Club's Easter meet. I have told you about the club before, but just to refresh your memory — we are the smallest croquet club in the world with a closed membership of twelve. We were incorporated on a Saturday afternoon in January 1992, and all those present on that day became members until death. My friend Paul who was present at the inaugural match and who has not played since — because he does not enjoy playing croquet — has tried to divest himself of membership many times. This is not permitted under the rules, and an apology on his behalf is registered at every annual general meeting. No new members can be admitted to the club, but we do have invited guest players at our matches. When we meet at Tommy's Cabin we play on the only tussock croquet lawns in the world, although we have not applied to register our lawns in the *Guinness Book of Records* so cannot verify this claim.

The club has a uniform and a motto. The official uniform is 'whites' and a blazer of any colour with the club monogram to be worn on the pocket. The club motto is 'keep your balls together' which in Latin is *tuo globi cunctum* something-or-other. We always play in pairs; when you play as a pair it is important to stick together so that one or other of you can harass the enemy, hence 'keep your balls together'. Croquet is a mean and nasty game. We do not often wear the official uniform. At most matches we have an exotic dress code for the day. The Easter meet code this year was British Raj.

Easter Monday was a celestial autumn day, the sky bright blue, the hills golden, the air unruffled and the sun mellow. We were a motley assortment of British *sahibs* and *memsahibs*, *maharajas* and *maharanis*. Wandering pig-shooters happening upon the tussock lawns would have thought us mad, but what is life if you cannot slip the bonds of self and assume an altogether other? Each one of us has a dress-up box at home, an essential requirement for being a member of the club. Harry and I are limited in our choice of costumes because I am not a natural hoarder, but some of our members are genetically predisposed to hoarding and they have trunks full of ancient and mothballed clothes. Harry's riding breeches and long black boots suit most historic occasions, which further advances my theory that the hunt is an anachronism, and I generally find something to waft about in.

On Monday we met at eleven, played a round or two then broke for tiffin. Everyone brought Indian food; *dhal*, *poppadums*, *chapattis*, rice and curry which we heated on the barbecue. I made *korma*. Well it wasn't really *korma*, as it should be made with lamb and I did not have any. I made it with beef. After the final match, which was played for the Golden Rose Bowl trophy, we served afternoon tea. We were a bit short on tea *wallahs*, so the winners of the annual TCCC thermette race were charged with heating the water in their antique NZ Rail thermette. A Tommy's Cabin Croquet Club afternoon tea is always served in fine porcelain china cups with saucers, the tea is poured from a silver teapot and the *petits fours* are served on a tiered cake stand; and there are, of course, tiny cucumber sandwiches. But I digress, the *korma* recipe. Before I give you the recipe I will tell you how I came by an authentic *korma* recipe.

The recipe came from our old school friend Robyn with whom I have remained in tenuous touch ever since leaving high school. After many years overseas, Robyn resurfaced in Wellington with a tall, dark handsome man from Rajasthan. While she was in Wellington Robyn taught Indian cookery. I would recommend that you to go to her cooking classes, but she has returned to Rajasthan where she and Manev manage an exclusive resort. Here is her recipe for *korma*.

Robyn's *Korma*

1kg diced lamb
1 tbsp ground coriander seeds
4 onions
1 tsp ground cumin seeds
6 cloves garlic
1 tsp chilli powder
1 tbsp shredded ginger
½ tsp cardamom
½ cup yoghurt
½ tsp cinnamon
3 tbsp oil and 1 tbsp butter
½ tsp turmeric
1 tsp salt (or more to taste)
½ tsp saffron strands soaked in 2 tbsp hot water
100g ground almonds or cashews

Grind coriander seeds, garlic, one onion and the almonds or cashews. Marinate the lamb pieces in this mixture for 2 hours. Heat the oil and butter together and slowly cook the onions until soft and golden. Add the remaining spices. Increase the heat and add the lamb. Stir-fry until all the moisture dries up. Reduce heat before adding the yoghurt. Beat the yoghurt and add slowly, by the tablespoon-full (you will curdle the gravy if you add it too quickly). Reduce to a slow simmer, cover and cook for 1½ hours. Add the saffron and the water in which it has soaked, then leave for a further hour for the saffron to permeate.

A note on spices. Robyn converted me into a fresh spice freak. It is so easy to have a drawer full of ancient spices that taste like stale cardboard. Throw them all away. I roast and grind my own coriander (home-grown), cumin and cardamom, I grate my own nutmeg, and I make sure I refresh my turmeric and other less-used spices at least once a year. I do not use the saffron, it's very expensive and I'm never sure whether I can taste it or not.

Dear Virginia

Ohmygawd! I am tired just reading about the effort you make to cook wonderful food in the country. Are we city people just lazier? Rarely do city people cook without convenient mixes, packets, sauces. Some of us even buy peeled and chopped vegetables. Robert's Auckland flatmate, Margot, runs a business chopping onions and packaging them for just these sorts of busy people. But, of course, they can't be more busy than you are.

(I must admit, though, that I save all my home-grown coriander seeds — and it grows like a weed — and roast all the seeds and use them in curries and with tomatoes. But I thought I was the only one who did this sort of crazy, time-wasting thing.)

This is the season for book launches. With food (and wine) prices on the up and up, a weekly book launch can supplement a poor writer's diet and prevent the symptoms of cold-turkey alcohol withdrawal as the GST-return season, and its associated belt-tightening, begins. So a good book launch is defined by its food and wine. Unity is the best provider. A unique Wellington scene, on a cold April evening, is office and shop workers huddled around the bus stops on Willis Street at 6.30, waiting to go home, and right beside them, the brightly-lit bookshop's doors flung open. The sounds of traffic mix with the gulps of laughter and clinking glasses. A necklace of buses comes around the corner and all the huddlers get on. In Unity, Tilly announces it is time for the inevitable speeches. Late commuters slump to the bus stop, knowing they've just missed the bus. And all Willis Street settles into hopeful expectation again: the tired commuter for his bus, the writer waiting for the speeches to end so he can grab that little *vol au vent* before a colleague does.

Dear Janice

I wasn't planning on writing a letter right now, but it has been forced upon me by circumstance. The circumstance is a culinary matter of grave importance. Harry attended his first hunt of the season today. A hunt begins at midday; after a briefing and a few nips from the old hip flask to bolster the nerves, the field sets off after the wily hare. The field is led by the Master who follows the Huntsman. The Huntsman is in charge of the hounds; he is assisted by two whips who help keep the hounds in order. Hounds must hunt as a pack, there is no room for individual intelligence amongst hounds. The whips stifle individualism amongst the pack. Harry sometimes whips with his smart bone-handled whip. The Brackenfield Huntsman is a man by the name of Daf, a bit of a legend in horse-riding circles (you can make of that what you will). Anyway, after the hunt there is a 'breakfast' which happens about three-thirty or four. All the riders must bring a 'plate' to contribute to the hunt breakfast. Daf reprimanded Harry for the standard of his plate, which is, indirectly, a reprimand of myself as the chef of the house. Harry took a packet of chocolate biscuits. I asked Harry if Daf was joking, and Harry said no, he was not.

I don't give a fig about the hunt, but I will not be reprimanded about the standard of the Double Tops plate. Harry's hunt breakfasts are simple: I usually send him off with a billy full of cheerios and a bottle of home-made tomato sauce. Harry takes a little gas stove and heats the cheerios (except they are not allowed to be called cheerios now — they are cocktail sausages — and butchers are not allowed to give them to children any more in case they are riddled with salmonella).

Hot cheerios are a very popular plate. Sometimes we don't have cheerios in the deep-freeze and I say to Harry, 'Buy a packet of chocolate biscuits' — but obviously, after a reprimand from the huntsman I will have to have something in reserve in the deep-freeze.

Daf and I have a fractious relationship on account of the fact I do not believe in hunting and often threaten to arrive on my bicycle. Daf once asked Harry where the bloody hell he got me from. I do not want him to feel sorrier for Harry than he does already, so I am going to make some cinnamon buns which I used to make in the days when I took the hunt plate much more seriously. When Fleur and Harry both hunted I used to make ham sandwiches, little iced cakes and cinnamon buns.

Dear Virginia

I am angry with Daf. I think you should use one of those docking rings on him, or put some dipping chemical in his hunt hip flask. Conscientious cooks like you do lay yourselves open to the misery of unrecognized effort. I experienced a version of it this weekend when I spent two hours making a *pissaladière* with a magnificent sunburst design on the top made out of anchovies. All this effort was wasted on the motorway when a truck shed a king-size mattress which landed right in front of the car. I jammed on the brakes and the beautiful *pissaladière* sailed through the air, raining onions and anchovies all over the front seats and the back of my head.

Instead of writing to you of a major culinary achievement equal to your hot cross buns and your *korma*, I am going to reply with a quick, simple dish. City people never have enough time to cook. This recipe is all about sassy appearance, but it's so easy it's like being a cheating hostess. A long time ago, friends Brian and Albert bought a large two-storey house in Auckland. It had a magnificent wide, curving staircase with carved balustrades. Brian said the rest of the house was quite ordinary. He said the place was 'fur coat and no knickers', meaning its glamour was superficial. This recipe is like that. It's a city thing.

Red Pepper Pasta

Grill 4 red peppers over the gas flame. Put them in a bag for a few minutes to absorb the heat, then remove them and rub the thin burnt layer off. Slice your peppers into strips. Remove the seeds. (If this all seems like too much of a hassle, you can buy prepared red peppers, all ready to go. They are on a supermarket shelf in glass jars. And another energy saver: if the barbie's up and running one night, give the peppers to the BBQ maestro with the long-handled tongs. He'll enjoy turning them over and over until they are nicely charred.) After you've sliced them, you can store them in the fridge until the day you want to use them.

So, the actual pre-dinner moment of preparation begins here:

Toast ¼ cup pine nuts. Don't burn them.

Cook 200g spaghetti.

To assemble the dish: mix the spaghetti with 100g crumbled feta or goat's cheese, some olives, the pine nuts and peppers.

Sprinkle on a little balsamic vinegar and olive oil. Add some coriander from the garden. (You don't need to grind it!) Make a salad too. *Voilà!*

If I leave work and become my own person, earning enough to survive on and no more, will I spend a lot of time perfecting complicated and wonderful dishes? I don't think so. I think I will still cheat with my own fast and flashy food.

In late April in my garden feijoas fall from the trees like a green hailstorm. I love feijoas. I love the smell of them in the house. I love the look of them when I arrange them like mice along the blue kitchen bench. I did this the other day, with a toy mouse (a cat toy) at each end of the line. A visiting child was entranced. And I love to eat them, of course.

A Quick Feijoa Dessert

On your way home, stop at the supermarket for cream and crystallized ginger (it's hiding in the bag-yourself section).

Scoop the pulp out of a pile of feijoas. Mash them in a bowl (maybe 2 cups) with 1 tbsp of honey and 1 tbsp of lemon juice. Or get someone else to mash them. Get a kid to whip the cream. Use half of a 500ml bottle, and then another dollop because it's irresistible to add a bit more.

Add crystallized ginger. If you want to add other things, especially if there are children eaters, try chopped-up chewy aeroplane lollies. Pile it all into a green bowl and put it in the fridge until everyone has finished their veggies.

Today I hauled the beans down from their sticks and poles and wires, an extraordinary amount of plant volume from one small pink seed. I cut the beans off above-ground and left the bean roots undisturbed to hibernate over the winter. I noticed snails clinging to the undersides of the tallest leaves. Is this bean-climbing an extreme sport for snails? I pulled one off its leaf, named it Jack, and threw it, gently, over the fence. I saw Ron in the terrace. He showed me his one-pound, one-ounce tomato. I just told him he had to modernize and go metric.

Robert is back in Auckland, awaiting a call to work in Canada. He is packing — crash helmet, iPod speakers, and All Black flag.

Dear Janice

Last week Harry was censured about his hunt breakfast plate, do you remember?

This Tuesday, the day before the hunt, I was about to make cinnamon buns to make amends, when I sliced my index finger on a newly sharpened vegetable knife. To stem the blood I wrapped the finger in tightly wadded rolls of Elastoplast. Elastoplast and bun-kneading are not a good idea. The plaster might get sucked from your finger by the sticky dough and someone could choke on it. I put the bun ingredients away. This did not solve the plate problem. I kept thinking about Harry saying to Daf 'You *are* joking', and Daf saying 'No, actually I'm not'.

I'm not sure whether Daf would have been joking. I do not know him well enough to know. It was as I was thinking about tea that a solution appeared. I would make *frittata*, one for tea and one for the hunt. I love *frittata*, or *eggah* as the Middle Eastern cook Claudia Roden calls them. You can throw almost anything in with the egg and it will taste good. I looked in the garden, the fridge and the pantry — new potatoes, buttercup pumpkin, feta cheese, manuka-smoked bacon, parsley and coriander — they would make a good *frittata*. This is what I did.

Frittata

First, I chopped six large Cliff's Kidney potatoes and a quarter of a pumpkin and I parboiled them in lightly salted water. Then I took two frying pans; in each I melted butter and olive oil together — the amount you use is entirely personal, some people have a fetish about too much butter. I tossed the pumpkin and potato along with the six chopped bacon rashers in the butter and fried them until the potato was softish.

In a very big bowl I beat 14 large farm eggs until they were frothy, I added half a teaspoon of salt and a lot of ground pepper. I poured half the egg mixture into each pan, and then I threw into each half a packet of cubed feta. On top of the egg mixture I sprinkled a couple of handfuls of mixed fresh coriander and parsley, and more ground black pepper. I turned the pans down to a very low heat, put a lid on top of each one and cooked them until they were set.

Then, onto the hunt *frittata* I drifted shaved Parmesan cheese. I placed both *frittata* under the grill where they puffed up and browned on top. We ate one for tea, the other I sent along to the hunt with Harry with strict instructions to make sure that Daf ate a slice.

I don't know why I went to so much trouble, Janice. I don't approve of hunting; pride, I suppose. Daf did not eat any of the *frittata*. Someone else ate it all before he got to the table, and I'm sure he would not have noticed had Harry presented with another packet of biscuits anyway. Harry hobbled home from the hunt like a cripple; a pony had kicked him in the knee right at the beginning of the day. He rode for the rest of the day without feeling any pain, but by the time he arrived home he was an invalid in need of tender care. I had to tug his boots off, pour him a whisky for the pain, and run him a bath. After the bath and a plate of shepherd's pie I wrapped his knee in ice for 10 minutes, made him sit with it elevated, dosed him with anti-inflammatory pills, assured him he would walk again, then put him to bed.

Dear Virginia

Oh! The waste of effort. A *frittata* that Daf didn't even see! I hope you took a photo of it and emailed it to him. I am still angry on your behalf. I am now indulging in licorice to keep the anger suppressed.

I guess the nearest equivalent I can think of is the office morning tea, where everyone is meant to bring something. And it is crucial that you bring the right thing. In the good old days — before project reports, spreadsheets and timesheets — people did indeed bring home-made cakes, sausage rolls, *rewena* bread, things they had taken trouble over. Now it is more slapdash. Everyone rushes over to New World and comes back with chippies, Cheezels, Mallowpuffs or Ginger Kisses. The Ministry's healthy eating strategy is rarely adhered to, although you can count on Tricia to always supply grapes.

The glorious weather continues. It is one thing to have a great summer and a long autumn and extended daylight saving. It is quite another order of the unprecedented to have a fine, hot, still Anzac Day. Extraordinary. I arrived at a family party that night, just as all the older soldiers were leaving to go home early, sheepishly mentioning the dawn service they'd attended and their being 'done in' by it.

The party was a typical Wellington mix of people. There were of course bureaucrats talking together, using their own mysterious language. One showed me his children's artwork —

in computer printouts he had brought with him. 'The trouble is, different printers result in different colours. I can't get the colours right.'

'Oh, my daughter could do that for you,' another said. 'She'll just throw it into PageMaker and . . .'

Young women, enthusiastic about their first office jobs, were talking about JDs (job descriptions) and salary scales. One told me she had learnt to do layered headings in a questionnaire. 'Cool,' another said. A young man from IRD was advising them to do an Excel training course.

There were Weta contractors, playing hacky sack and talking quietly about armatures. There were a few teachers, life coaches, counsellors, and people running their own businesses as artists or, more mysteriously, trainers. There were IT guys talking about model aircraft, and Gareth Morgan employees chatting up the young bureaucrats. At these sorts of gatherings there is always someone who's written a book or has an idea for one. There's always someone who's written a song and wants to sing it to you right then and there.

Tonight some people were talking about farmers they know. It is a status symbol, knowing people who have a farm you can go and stay on. The farm should be close to a ski field and hot springs. It's essential it is also near a winery, good restaurants, and has cellphone coverage. A brother-in-law has such friends, and was impressing a group of Weta contractors with descriptions of shearing and four-wheel-drive tracks.

And I wonder — how do we end up where we do in life? So much of it is to do with serendipitous meetings, marriages, job placements, getting in the wrong queue. (Do you remember when we met at the school reunion and Robin told everyone that she only ended up doing commerce — and becoming a top bureaucrat — because she got in the wrong queue on enrolment day at university and signed up for a commerce degree and not the arts degree she'd planned to do?) And how do we keep going? And why, in this small country, do most people live urban lives, mustered by mortgage mavens, and yet hanker for the more 'real' crumpled landscapes of the Southern Alps, about which they know nothing? Would we know a cryptorchid from a cow? Or from an orchid? Course not. But I think to myself, remembering what you told me years ago: just drive life's gravel roads as though a sheep truck was coming around every bend and you'll get to the end safely, if undramatically.

Anyway, this gathering was a well-organized barbeque with delicious meat and large tables to sit at. I dislike BBQs where the meat is not good steak, and is curled up at the ends, unappetizing and chewy. There are never sharp, serrated steak knives to cut it up with, and rarely tables on which to do this, even if you are offered such an implement. The effect is that everyone is chewing and chewing and totally unable to network with each other — the thing they are all at the BBQ to do. Everyone is juggling a plate and a glass and cutlery. People perch on the rims of big pot plants, or are cast, unable to get out of damp deck chairs. Dogs love barbeques because of the manna that rains down from heaven in the form of gristle, chop bones and bread crusts. But there was no dog at this gathering. The memory of Bunsen being fed far too many chops by all the family's little children, and having to spend the next day at the vet's, did flash across my mind.

When I got home, an email told me we have won a contract to make an educational CD-ROM for the Dairy Board to distribute to schools. The CD-ROM has a talking cow who gives you milk to fuel your spaceship en route back from the Milky (it gets worse, be warned) Whey.

May

Dear Janice

We were picking grapes today at the Over the Hill vineyard. All our fellow pickers talked of flying off to warmer climes to escape the worst of the winter; they are like swallows flitting off when the days grow short. We will winter-over, like drab little sparrows hoping the sun will shine again. The leaves are falling from the birches in drifts, and frost stalks the mornings. It will be a long winter. There is only gloom and doom on sheep farms this autumn, and the magpies are oodle-wardling in the bare branches of the trees. I will have to do lots of cooking to keep the cold and the gloom at bay.

Tonight when we arrived home I heard an owl cry in the pine plantation, an eerie wail, like a harbinger of doom. I've never seen an owl: I tried to surprise it in the branches of the trees, and every time I crept close its cry came from a further tree until I reached a clearing and stood still. It screeched again and again, and then I saw a bird, dark against the dying sky, fly from the pines into the dusk and I heard it no more.

Dear Virginia

Do not worry about owls. We used to hear them every night on Tinakori Hill, until the council pulled all the trees out using a Sikorsky helicopter that nearly shook the house from its foundations when it flew over. The owls have disappeared. I miss their deep, sad hooting. If owls bring doom and gloom, then the removal of the owls from the hill would have changed my life forever. I would have taken up partying and become irrepressible. I haven't noticed anything less gloomy since the owls' departure; just a torn, scarred hill.

I had to buy lamb this week because I was feeding a Californian actor. Foreigners all want to eat our lamb. They think it's our national dish. 'No,' I explained to David, the actor, 'our national dish is pumpkin soup, especially with coconut cream. But I will cook you lamb on Sunday. The last time I ate lamb was when I was eating at Double Tops where Virginia cooked the most delicious lamb ever.'

But that was farm kill. That meat would never have sat around in a supermarket chiller on an absorbent pad and covered in plastic. Supermarket lamb is very expensive and it comes in two forms — leg of, and chops. I wanted to make your slow-cooked Persian stew with cumin and ginger and loads of parsley, garlic and coriander from the garden. Hmm. I decided on neck chops — the cheapest. They'd be nice and gelatinous after slow cooking, and they'd hold those flavours. I fought the crowds to the checkout. At home I marinated the chops in all the herbs and spices on a bed of chopped onion, then stowed it in the fridge. Then I changed and went out to dinner — to an ex-workmate's, Steve, and his Mexican wife. She made *tortillas*, beans and rice. We talked about how nice it is to eat with your fingers and forget forks. I thought that, on Sunday, we could dip Moroccan bread into the lamb broth, and forget the rice. That tearing and dipping would be more visceral than eating rice with a fork.

But before I tell you about Sunday, I must tell you about

Steve's grandmother. At her 100th birthday party, the big moment was opening her stack of cards. The one on the top was big and beautiful, a very fine card. It came from the Queen and met with Steve's grandma's approval.

'Put it up there.' She pointed to the mantelpiece.

The second card was also big, beautiful and much admired. It came from the Governor-General. The third card, however, was not a card that had a crease down the middle, that you could open. It was just one small flat thing, like a certificate.

'Hmm. That's a certificate, not a card,' his grandma rumbled. 'Who's it from?'

'Our Prime Minister.'

'Don't display that one.'

The fourth card wasn't a card or even a certificate.

'A window envelope! For a birthday card!' She was outraged. She turned it over, unopened. On the back was a stamp from the office of Peter Dunne, her electorate MP.

'Throw that in the bin.'

Sunday morning, my niece from Auckland, Kerri, and I walked along the waterfront to Zarbo's for brunch. She was down in Wellington with girlfriends for a shopping expedition. Then I scampered home to prepare the slow-cooked Persian lamb stew. I made a salad from the garden — grated carrot, grated apple, chives, with walnuts from Alison's huge tree.

The Californian actor, who is here for six weeks to direct a grisly Pinter play, told me after a few pre-dinner drinks — during which we ate up all the Moroccan bread and the guacamole — that his wife, back in California, is eleven weeks pregnant. This called for more wine. This is where the benefit of slow food-cooking comes in. I could forget the meal. It was just sitting there, glugging occasionally. All I had to do was cook the now necessary rice — 2 cups of long grain rice to 3 cups of water. 15 minutes of cooking, then 10 minutes of standing with the lid still on. So my excessive wine intake didn't spoil the dinner. And my guest didn't feel I was more interested in the progress of my cooking than in the progress of his progeny. A cook/hostess has to be totally focused on her guests. You can't be making *soufflés* or pancakes, or even Yorkshire pudding, when you are entertaining. The food has to appear by miraculous sleight of hand. No effort must be apparent.

I threw the rice on and it just bubbled away. We moved to the dining room. I turned the rice off and left it while we sorted out more wine and new glasses and serviettes. I tossed the salad. And when we finally ate the stew — about an hour later than planned — it was still perfectly delicious. We toasted the child again and again, and David told me their child will eat only pure food. I didn't say, 'Yeah, right.' It seemed the wrong note on which to end a good meal.

Dear Janice

No, no, no, Janice, you must find a butcher from whom to buy your lamb. I'm sure that butcher meat is more like home kill than supermarket meat. Butchers take more care selecting their animals, and when they butcher the carcass they don't pack all the cuts on little black polystyrene trays which have to be recycled. Supermarket meat is menstrual, it leaks blood into absorbent pads that have to be thrown away. It's yucky and wasteful. Find yourself a butcher! All the same, I'm pleased you cooked my lamb dish and that it was a success.

Speaking of meat, your cow 'Janice' is worth a thousand dollars on the hooks. Harry reminds me often of her dollar value and I do not hear him. I tell him she is in calf, that she will be a wonderful mother and will pay for herself many times over by popping out a calf a year. Today she had her TB sensitivity injection, on Thursday the test will be read. TB testing is a yearly millstone. I do mean millstone and not milestone. Harry and I have spent the last week mustering the cows and calves down from the hills. Today we ushered 650 animals through the cattle yards. Each animal is injected underneath the tail; three days later, the tester will return and he will run his fingers beneath the tails of the 650 animals to feel for lumps. A lump means TB and the cow or calf is slaughtered. We have not had a TB case for five years, so it is very unlikely that Janice will have to be slaughtered.

Janice did not walk up the race like a common cow. She stood in the back pen and the tester came to her. I rubbed her head while Warwick injected her tail. Afterwards I escorted Janice and her friend Doris — the wild and dangerous Doris, the calf — to the back paddock where they will graze until the reading. Janice does not associate with ordinary cows. She and Doris met last year. Doris was a pet calf six years ago. She was very wild and often charged me — and the milk bucket — soaking me with warm, sticky milk. As soon as Doris was old enough to fend for herself, she joined the main herd. She reared two good calves, but last year she lost condition and returned to the paddocks with a couple of very elderly cows. Janice spent the summer with them, and she and Doris became friends. I like to think they discussed their childhoods and realized they had shared the same foster mother, me. Doris has been so much more affable since she and Janice have been friendly. Janice must have told her that I wasn't really a bad mother.

I'm tired from mustering cows. As you get the herds closer to the yards the cows become more reluctant to move forwards and they fight the dogs. A cow with calf is a fearsome beast when she is bothered by a dog. If the dog seeks respite behind you, you are faced with a raging, snorting, maniac cow charging dangerously, with head lowered trying to beat up the dog. You must call the cow's bluff and charge forwards with your mustering stick. Never let a cow get the better of you. It is all very tiring and so I'm off to bed.

Dear Virginia

I'm writing this in the early morning. I have a hot-water bottle on my lap to prevent hypothermia. Heaters in the sitting room and the study are beginning their day's work. The house will be just warm enough by bedtime, when we will turn them off. Outside everything is white with rain — the sky, the hill. The sound of it on the roof means playing music is impossible. I'm sitting at the computer in the attic (heat will rise, won't it?), writing to you about going to the Arctic.

At 4.30am Margot, Robert's flatmate, texted me. She and Lennon, Robert's guitar mate, were in the check-in queue at the airport and she was holding Robert's hand and he was nervous. I texted Robert goodbye. I'm a slow texter in the middle of the night. He replied saying he'd got through Customs and was waiting for his flight, one of many flights that will take him to Yellowknife, North West Territories of Canada. From there he'll be assigned to a Far North helicopter base. I'd looked at the company's possible bases on Google Earth. Could be Fort

Lizard — a square of razed ground with one building for a helicopter, and another small shed for, presumably, the pilot to hang his hammock up and haul out his guitar. 'I'll just take the acoustic,' he'd told me yesterday. 'It's not the place for the electric.'

Last night the flatmates and ex-flatmates had gathered for a farewell meal — a roast. Roasts seem to have become a tradition in the flat. I wondered if Robert in the check-in queue, with all those travellers and his whole future in front of him, was as nervous as he had been several weeks ago when he'd phoned to say Gerald and Olive were coming to dinner and he, Robert, was on roast potato watch. Gerald and Olive are Irish. The potatoes had to be perfect.

By now Margot will have returned to the empty flat, such a boy place — guitars, a huge sound system, flat-screen TV and three couches — and I'm coping with a mother's thoughts on such occasions. Always the same for all of us. We just want them to be happy.

Dear Janice

I remember the morning when Fleur left for a year away in Britain, our only child departing the country. I remember the terrible bereft feeling. No matter how old, mature, grown-up our children become, they are still children and you still worry about them. I make a point of every goodbye being a goodbye I will remember, in case it is the last. Not something I considered before Cave Creek, but it is so very important because that will be the last memory you have if they don't come back. Not that you should ever think in terms of someone not coming back — but it is prudent to take the precaution of a goodbye being a happy one. I well remember the last time I waved goodbye to Kit. We were waiting in the dodgy corner of Cathedral Square for a bus that was late. I kept saying, 'We must have missed the bus', and Kit would say, 'No Mum, it's a West Coast bus — it's always late.' There was a drunk man trying to sleep on a bench in the bus shelter, he kept rolling off. When the bus finally pulled away from the square, half an hour late, Kit looked from the window with a wide smile and waved. It was a happy goodbye. I hope the goodbyes were good, and I'm sure Robert will be perfectly safe and return at the end of his employment contract with lots of money and valuable experience in piloting helicopters.

Dear Virginia

The idea of Robert with lots of money is one of those inherent contradictions that make me smile. Like you in the vineyard, I'm thinking of all my friends who are, or have just, or are about to, globally roam.

There's David and Tricia. I spent the weekend with them in Greytown. They leave on Wednesday for their walking tour in France and a week in New York. A lot of the conversation over dinner that night was about boots. Sam, a potter son of Masterton friends, has just been asked to go to Northern China to make huge ceramic eels and have them cast in bronze. Helen and Tim have a new grandchild, their fifth. They are off to Canberra to see him. David the sound engineer phoned yesterday. He's just back from Guatamala and Mexico. Keith and Diana are taking their bikes to Romania so they can bike through the countryside and look into people's gardens. Jane tumbled off a flight yesterday, safely returning all of the twenty-three kids she took on a school trip to Paris and the south of France. That's just the globe-trotting news of this weekend.

For me the journey back from Greytown in sleeting rain was enough global roaming for now. The train turned into a bus in Upper Hutt. 'No trains to Wellington today,' the conductor announced and everyone accepted this without comment. The bus was so cold that the metal handrail felt sticky. Teenagers screamed behind me about their cloud breath. I suspected Fort Lizard in Canada's Far North wouldn't be this grim.

Dear Janice

So all your friends are chasing the sun and leaving for the other side of the world. Someone has to stay at home and earn the foreign exchange to pay for their holidays; that's us. As we muster the hills, the sky above us is traversed with vapour trails; I wonder what the detritus of the jet engines is doing to the sky. I feel virtuous standing there on my small carbon footprint in the grass. We don't do holidays; Harry thinks he's on holiday every day, and I've got used to sharing his point of view. We have twice flown to Sydney for the weekend, but that is the outer reach of our travelling.

Dear Virginia

May is when certain city people, craving the old country ways, go out scrumping. I think it's an old English word. These days you don't hop over the fence and grab the squire's apples. You drive into the country and take whatever food you can find from berms, walking tracks, dunes, and long-abandoned gardens.

Greytown is excellent for scrumping. When we arrived at lunchtime on Saturday, we parked beside the supermarket in order to walk across the road to the French Bakery to get bread, and an almond croissant or two as a treat. But I was distracted by the tree in the parking lot. It is huge, the sort of English tree Queen Elizabeth the First would have sat under if she'd come to New Zealand. It is a walnut tree. Under it were hundreds of walnuts. We collected some, then walked through the alley to West Street along the side of a fenced-off section that was empty except for one giant feijoa tree and a large sign: *Private Property, Keep Out.* Under the tree, hundreds of feijoas made it look like a green boulder bank. A young girl — about ten — looked warily at us, sussed out that we didn't look like the owners of the sign, then said, in ringing tones, to her friends, 'I'm just going into my private property to get some feijoas.' She climbed the fence and began scrumping.

In Wood Street there's a massive chestnut tree. Under it were burnished, red-brown chestnuts. We gathered a bag of them, too, pushing Zephyr the dog out of the way so he didn't pee on them. He tends to do this on any object we are looking closely at. He's not the best scrumping dog. David told us that he'd stopped with Z at an intersection where a mother and daughter were waiting with the daughter's pink tricycle. While the mother looked left and right, checking for speeding SUVs,

Z did a quick squirt all over the seat of the tricycle. This is the sort of behaviours that can give dogs a bad name in towns.

Dear Janice

I cannot grow my own walnuts, but I swap the walnuts with my friend Oonah for marmalade and chocolates and other home-made stuff, so I think this recipe qualifies as almost using my own garden produce. Walnuts should always be used straight from the shell. If you buy walnuts already opened and chopped they will most likely have a bitter, rancid taste.

Cheesy Walnut Biscuits

100g softened butter
125g aged cheddar cheese or half cheddar and
    half blue
125g plain flour
large pinch cayenne
100g freshly shelled chopped walnuts
1 egg for glazing

Put the butter, cheese, flour and cayenne in the food processor and whizz until a dough forms. Remove from the processor and knead the dough to remove any air pockets. Shape the dough into a sausage, or a narrow rectangle if you want square biscuits, then wrap in cling-film and put in the fridge for a minimum of 1 hour.

To bake, unwrap the dough and with a sharp knife cut into thin slices. Place on oven trays covered with baking

paper, brush the biscuits with beaten egg, and sprinkle with
a generous covering of finely chopped walnuts.

Bake at 180 degrees.

Dear Virginia

I like your walnut biscuits recipe. If I go scrumping again, I will
make the biscuits. David and Alison, from the lifestyle block,
pickle the walnuts on their tree, but they say the process is
fiddly and time-consuming. So pickling is not for me.

Dear Janice

I've never been scrumping. As kids we went stealing fruit around
the orchards of Manutuke. In the summer I used to crawl out
my bedroom window long after dark to meet Jill and Ken on the
Papatu Road. We met to go 'raiding'. We jogged up the warm
tar-seal road, leaping into the ditches if a car drove by, until we
reached the orchards. We had scrumples (that's a word meaning
scruples when scrumping). We didn't steal from the widow, or
the generous orchardists who gave fruit away; we stole from the
mingy orchardist. We raided his watermelon patch, crawling
under the hedge to grab huge, striped watermelons. I can still
taste the warm, sweet stickiness of sun-ripened watermelon as
we lay sucking the rinds in the middle of the warm, dark road
amidst a chorus of singing crickets.

Down here in the hills back of Hawarden we are much more genteel: we go foraging. Our forage foods — field mushrooms and road-side apples — are coming to an end with the onset of the frost season. Mushrooms hibernate at the whiff of a frost, and apples drop from the trees to rot in the long grass. I do not know what the city equivalent of forage foods is. Do you ever go foraging in Thorndon? Do you forage outside the goods depots at supermarkets for food and vegetables tossed because they are past their use-by date?

Field mushrooms really do grow in fairy rings; sometimes you find a complete circle, but most often they grow in crescents. Mushrooms are irresistible: when you see them dotted in small white daubs amongst the green grass you are drawn to pick them. I'm usually shifting sheep when I see mushrooms, and I stop and fill my canvas hat with the small fresh ones. To pick a new mushroom and turn it over is to gaze upon perfection. The pale-pink gills are fluted in the most exquisite symmetry you will ever see.

I can't explain why I love them so much, maybe it is because their perfect beauty is transitory. As soon as you pick a mushroom the pink begins to dull and turn fawn, it browns and then it blackens. Cooking mushrooms is not a crime, they would have frizzled anyway. I don't like fried or grilled mushrooms, the slimy feel in my mouth is repugnant; but I love mushroom soup. If you make a soup with pink mushrooms it turns the palest shade of purple/pink grey.

Field Mushroom Soup

Pick a canvas hatful of small field mushrooms with pink gills. Wash and peel the mushrooms then slice them in thin slices or chunks. Gently fry in 25g butter.

In another saucepan make a white sauce. Melt 50g butter

and stir in 2 tbsp of flour to make a *roux*. (A *roux* is the name for a blend of flour and fat, cooked gently.) Cook the *roux* for 2 minutes, stirring to prevent it sticking on the bottom of the pan. Then add, very gradually, 1 cup of milk. 'Gradually' means little pours at a time and stirring until each pour thickens, that way your sauce will never go lumpy.

When all the milk has been added and the sauce is thick, blended and simmering, you can add the fried mushrooms. If you like a rich soup, you can thin the mixture to soup consistency with milk. If you are worried about fat, cholesterol and other dietary evils that could kill you, you can thin it with water. I always thin my mushroom soup with blue-top milk.

After the consistency is right, season with salt and ground pepper. If you don't like the idea of mushroom lumps catching in your teeth, you can throw the soup in the blender and pulverize it. Last time I made mushroom soup I served it sprinkled with chopped coriander.

A note on the white sauce: the method described here was taught to me in cooking classes at Central School by the fearsome Mrs Lincoln. We girls were all very afraid of Mrs Lincoln and we obeyed her every instruction. We beat our butter and sugar until it was creamy pale, we whisked egg whites to a froth that stuck in the bowl if you tipped it upside down, we folded and rolled our flaky pastry five times over to create crispy pie crusts. We cut the butter into the flour for scones until the mixture resembled the finest breadcrumbs.

Dear Virginia

What would Mrs Lincoln have thought of Greytown David, I wonder? On Monday, David in Greytown got back from his morning dog walk and put his weekly eggs in a saucepan and on the stove to hard-boil. Eight eggs, two per day for four days. Then he did a few things, then a few more, then went back to writing his next book. One hour later he noticed a funny smell and thought, 'Hmmm, someone's burning something — maybe at the Workingmen's Club down the road.' Another hour went by. Much hard work was done. The smell was beginning to make concentrated thinking impossible, however. David went 'Hmmm', then he said 'Oh shit!' He followed his nose and found the cause of the smell, in his own kitchen, not in the Workingmen's Club. He dashed around the house with this very hot saucepan for a while. Where to put it? Where to put it? Then he flung it outside on his pebble-garden stones to cool down. He left the eggs in their ruined saucepan, rock-hard and bursting from their shells, and thought he'd get rid of them some time.

The next day the smell was still all through his house. The saucepan had at last cooled. He looked at the blackened mess, and left it. The next morning he went out there to check on them and — guess what? No eggs. No shells. Empty black saucepan. Traces of shell all over the back garden. Zephyr, poor dog, was lying in the shed looking as though he'd been turned to concrete. David emailed: *He hasn't done a poo yet today. He may not do one for a week. But the shells should do his bones no end of good.*

Although the story is funny, to me the disturbing phrase is: 'put his weekly eggs on . . . to hard-boil'. David is a lovely man whose partner works in Wellington, Monday to Friday. She returns to Greytown on Friday night's train, to a man almost gravid with eggs, who is presumably delighted to see her so long as she doesn't cook him an omelette.

Dear Janice

Women can burn pots, too; it is not a particularly male trait. They say it is an early sign of Alzheimer's, forgetting pots on the stove — but if this is so I have been suffering from it almost since infancy. My friend Alison once made the mistake of telling a table full of diners that she had burnt a pot whilst she was talking on the phone. She said that the best method of cleaning a severely burnt pot was to bury it in the garden for a while. Alison is known for her love of the telephone, and somehow the burnt-pot story was stretched into a rumour that her vegetable garden was so full of buried pots that there was no room to plant the summer crop. Tell your friend who burns boiled eggs to bury the pot in the garden for six months.

Dear Virginia

There's a lot of synchronicity happening at the moment. My friend Alison, from Paekakariki, has just rung to say — you guessed it: they are going overseas for a while. Norman up the road from them is going to take the chickens. He likes them running around his paddocks, apparently. The second strange synchronicity was that she said she had to put the phone down and open the oven because she had trays of walnuts slowly roasting in there and had to check them.

So I asked her what she does with them. After they've fallen from the tree, she and David and anyone else they can dragoon pick them up. The walnuts have to dry out on windowsills, or on trays for about a week until they are dry. Then it is shelling time. You hold the walnut up with the sharp end at the bottom. Insert a knife at the top end, between the lips — the black line that goes around the walnut. Twist the knife. Wiggle the shell off. The idea is to end up with one whole walnut, not a pile of pieces of walnut. You put them on trays and into the oven which is on 100. Alison keeps the door open slightly. When they are roasted but not burnt or dried out, take them out and put them into jars. Lots of jars, if you are Alison. She says that right now she is roasting three oven trays, piled two deep on each tray.

I heard another disastrous cooking story yesterday. Simon is a clever man. He is the operating systems guy at work, and very competent. At home, he is a totally different animal. This is the sorry tale of how Simon's wife, Robin, nipped out to the dairy and arrived home to find the remains of a fire in the sitting room and Simon lying in the doorway stabbed in the upper arm. This is what happened. When Robin went to the dairy, Simon decided he'd surprise her by making a *fondue* dinner. He found the *fondue* set, put it on the table, then carefully filled the meths burner. This is a tricky thing to do and, yes, he did spill some on the polished wooden table. He rushed to the sink to get a cloth, wiped the meths up, threw the cloth back into the sink. Phew. Crisis averted. Table saved. She would never know.

He lit the little burner and the table caught fire. Everywhere he'd wiped with the cloth, flames sprang up. Manfully, he tried to pat them out. He grabbed the cloth from the sink again — not thinking straight — wet it, wiped the table, and the fire got worse. But he was a practical bloke. He managed to contain the fire in the cloth. All he had to do now was to take the cloth of fire outside. It was in his right hand. He grabbed one of those long, skinny *fondue* forks in his left. He does not know why he grabbed the *fondue* fork. Maybe it was something subliminal to do with fire, the devil, fork — who knows? He rushed for the French doors. There were boxes in the way. He's an athletic sort of guy. He leapt over them and somehow caught the corner of the doorframe with the elbow of his left hand, the hand holding the *fondue* fork. This meant his forearm moved very quickly towards him and he stabbed himself in the upper arm with the fork.

'Hello, dear,' said Robin, coming through the door. 'What the . . . ?'

Dear Janice

What the . . . ? Is Simon a baby boomer? All baby boomers received *fondue* sets as wedding presents, used them once and then put them away in a cupboard. Why did he get it out again, I wonder — such a dangerous thing to do.

The forage apple trees grow on the banks on the side of the Virginia Road. Most of the apple trees are scattered between Double Tops and Melrose. I don't know why this is. Is the ground more suited to apple trees? Did the Rutherford children throw their apple cores out of the car window, or did visitors feel a need to munch an apple as they left civilization? All the apples are 'sports', which is the name for a pip-grown apple. Known apple breeds and commercial apples are grafted on to root-stock. Pips seldom breed true to their parent apple. All the Virginia Road apples are odd; I have sampled them on my bike rides. Some are bitter, and others sweet yet somehow tasteless; they are all small. I have found a late-season small red apple not far from the Kirdys' corner gate; the apples are sweet with a tart tang and don't mush when they are cooked. I baked an open tart with the apples last Sunday night.

Kirdy's Corner Apple Tart

Roll out a sheet of puff pastry and cut out a circle the size of a dinner plate, or cut two smaller circles. Place the pastry circles on baking paper. I spread the pastry with a thin layer of marzipan — because I happened to have some left over from a Simnel cake I didn't make. Peel, core and halve the apples and cut them into slices. Place them in ever increasing circles on top of the pastry. Brush with melted apricot jam glaze. Bake at 200 degrees for approximately 15 minutes. Take the tart out of the oven and glaze it again with apricot jam. Serve the tart hot with whipped cream or ice cream, and bugger the cholesterol.

Dear Virginia

I have just got back from having a dinner in Auckland where the tuna was seared on a hot stone at the table. (I fear Health and Safety issues here. This practice would not be allowed in the staff room.) After a red-eye flight home this morning and straight to work, I am too tired to write properly, but I must let you know the latest Greytown food alert! Tricia's cat is participating in a Forest and Bird study of what cats hunt. Tricia has to keep all cat kill in her freezer until it is collected by F and B. She has to be careful when looking for ice cream in the freezer and lives in fear of serving mouse mousse.

Hello, Janice

Not only are you a lady who lunches, you are also a dame who dines. I don't know how you keep up with all this dining and wining and lunching — I would be quite worn out and the size of a jumbo balloon. As for flying to Auckland for dinner, it has no parallel in my life. Though I have never travelled such a distance to dine I have gone to great lengths to lunch, but that is an entirely different matter. Let me tell you about it.

Some years ago we found ourselves owing ski friends Bob and Mary several meals on account of our stopping in at their farm on the way home from skiing. We decided we would host them to lunch at the ski field to clear the slate. We planned lunch on the top of Mount Terako. We talked with Doug and Jenny, who own the Mount Lyford Ski Field on the slopes of Mount Terako; they thought it would be fun, so we asked them and their Labrador Sophie to join us. We asked skiing friends Bill and Frank and Bruce; we asked their wives, too, but the thought of lunch on the top of Mount Terako somehow did not hold a huge social cachet for the wives. Or maybe it was that there was the small problem of getting there.

The invitation read *Black Tie*. On the beautifully calm, clear day of the luncheon, we assembled at the bottom of the Terako rope tow with two tables, nine chairs, white table-cloths, a candelabra, a bunch of daffodils and a crystal vase, a half dozen bottles of champagne and, of course, the lunch. The men wore dinner suits and the women wore long dresses. We carried all the gear up the rope tow to the get-off point, then we had to climb to the plateau on the top of the mountain.

This morning I got the photos out to remind myself of the day. There we all sit on the summit of the mountain with a cloud-streaked blue sky above us and trampled white snow beneath our feet; rugged grey mountains topped with snow stretch into the distance. We are sitting at a damask-covered table with a bunch of flowers in a vase and a candelabra with candles. The chairs have sunk a little into the snow. We are drinking champagne from fluted glasses, and Bill the waiter hovers, white serviette draped over one arm and a champagne bottle in the other. Sophie the Labrador lies in the snow; she ran to the top of the mountain beside Jenny as she rode the tow in a very slinky little black-and-gold evening number. The luncheon is a cold compilation of roast chicken, French bread, green salad, *Camembert* cheese, olives and fruit cheese followed by coffee, chocolates, grapes and fudge cake.

After lunch the air grew chilly, so we packed up. We did not ski down the steep shirt-front but descended the way we came, skiing down beside the rope tow. Skiing down a steep, snowy slope in a long red frock while carrying a white plastic chair made for a tricky ski run. The champagne was a definite aid to verve and courage. I did not fall.

Dear Virginia

The Auckland travel was a business trip. Do farmers have business trips, complete with business lunches or dinners? Probably not. Maybe there are a few perks to working in an office. But then I look at the five pairs of pantyhose dripping over the shower rail on this wet Saturday morning, and can't think of anything in my day in the office that can compare with the marvel of the Black Tie lunch on top of Mount Terako. Seared tuna at the Viaduct Basin isn't in the same league.

I am slowly unwinding after the horrors of a week of bad language. My intake of licorice and scorched almonds has soared to health-endangering levels. I am getting so very tired of office-speak. There was Tuesday's email containing arcane pseudo-academic gobbledegook: *the importance of distinctness of phonological representations of lexical items.* Does this mean 'reading out loud clearly'? Then there was the badly constructed sentence: *Brainstorm ideas with your students and provide opportunities to execute them.*

And it isn't just in the office where terrible language bombards me. Yesterday someone sent me an example of the worst sort of children's book. It was American, and called *The Stray Bullet.* It tells the sorry tale of the trajectory of a cute, shaggy baby bullet as she flies over a rainbow-hued landscape and tries desperately not to do harm. The cute little bullet would far rather stay at home in her gun than be sent out to commit mayhem:

> If I land in someone
> Not only do I hurt or kill them
> But I also hurt and die too.

The author, I noticed, was a Fijian. Obviously coup leaders in

Fiji didn't read the book at a formative time in their literacy development.

The office had a team-building day to end the week. I guess we would categorize your ski lunch as 'team building' if we were filling in weekly timesheets. We did clay-pigeon shooting on our day. We didn't sit on top of a mountain in ball dresses. But we did end up at the Wellesley Club for a feed. On the menu was: *Marinated lamb rump astride a field mushroom.* This seems to me to be a suitable last comment on a month full of lamb and mushrooms and murdered language.

June

Dear Virginia

It is pouring with rain here. The gutters are blocked with my neighbour's leaves. The water is pouring off the roof and down the windows.

A friend, Rachel, has recently moved back into the family home after a marriage break-up. She is celebrating having her own larder again by inviting some women friends round. We all have to take a dish from our own cultures — 'some food our mothers made' is how I interpret that. I'm thinking of Lancashire Hot Pot.

'Oh, no,' says Rachel. 'It has to be vegetarian.'

I am not a vegetarian, and I don't think I thrive best on all-vegetarian food. In my (cold-climate) culture we eat meat, as all cold-weather cultures always have. A family's main meal always has some small amount of meat or fish, or is cooked in animal fat (like Yorkshire pudding). I won't eat meat that's had a wretched and unnatural life as a living animal. I don't eat pork for that reason, unless it's wild pork or organic pork. But a sheep or cattle beast grazing your paddocks all its life — it doesn't seem to me that it had a bad life. I can eat that.

Hello, Janice

Out here at Double Tops the larder is a farm vehicle (Lada) and we store food in the pantry.

Now that it is winter I think you need to try making cinnamon buns. If you remember I made them for Harry to take to the hunt breakfast, but forgot to write down how I made them. This Saturday I made them again and I recorded everything, ingredients, method, times, temperatures, the lot. The recipe is a large one, it makes four dozen buns. I suggest you halve it.

Brackenfield Buns

Warm 2½ cups of milk to bath heat and add 1 tbsp of sugar and 50g of Surebake yeast. Wait 5 minutes until the yeast begins to froth. Pour the warm mixture into a bowl containing 1½ cups of fine flour, stir until smooth (the mixture will be quite sloppy). Cover the bowl with a damp tea towel and leave for half an hour.

In another bowl, cream 250g of butter and ¼ cup of sugar until light and creamy. Stir the creamed mixture into the dough and add 2 beaten eggs. When the butter and eggs are blended in to the dough, add 2½ cups of flour, stir with a wooden spoon until the mixture is well blended, and then very slowly mix in by degrees another cup of flour. You may not need all this flour, just add enough to render the dough elastic enough to knead. Tip out on to a bench and knead until the dough is smooth and shiny — about 10 minutes. Cover with the tea towel again — leave in a warm place until it doubles in size.

Then divide the dough in half, and roll out each half to ¼ inch thick. Spread with melted butter and sprinkle with a mixture of sugar and cinnamon. A good cinnamon mix is

2 tbsp of cinnamon to 1 cup of sugar. Roll the dough into a sausage, slice the sausage into buns, and place on baking paper in a meat dish. Leave the buns to rise to double in size — they should run into each other.

Bake at 200 degrees for 10 minutes, turn down to 180 and bake another 5 minutes. Baking times vary. I have a new oven — in my old oven I couldn't bake these buns at 200 degrees for 10 minutes, they would have burned; in my new oven 10 minutes at 200 is fine. You have to bake flexibly.

Your friends will love to visit when you bake Brackenfield Buns. Alternatively, take the buns out visiting; either way, the two dozen buns will vanish. Or you could just quarter the recipe.

Dear Virginia

Yes, I've just received Rachel's invitation. It is called a pantry party on the invite. A brother-in-law saw the invitation and thought it said panty party.

June is very cold this year, and we've had lots of sleety rain, so the only way to cope is to invite people to dinner. That way I don't have to go out in the cold, and I can drink as much as I want to because I won't be driving home.

On Thursday Bill and Yura, a Russian student, drove down from Raurimu. I offered them afternoon tea with Louise cake, kindly made by Jane Riley and given to me the night before when I ate English roast beef and Yorkshire pudding at their place. Phil Riley is a Yorkshireman and he knows how to make Yorkshire pud.

Bill didn't bring me a cream sponge this time. (Last time he stayed he arrived with a box, inside which, carefully wrapped, was one of his trademark perfect cream sponges, with a jar of cream and another of jam for the filling.) This time I had a surprise for them. I made a Russian dinner — complete with *borscht*.

There are many recipes for this Russian winter soup, but I didn't want a blenderized pink version with an island of sour cream on top. I wanted authentic. So I reached for *Lift the Lid of the Cumin Jar*, a wonderful book, published by the Wellington Home Tutor Scheme, in which immigrant women tell their stories and share their recipes. I followed the recipe of Luba, a Ukrainian. It was the first time I've ever grated beetroot. The kitchen looked like an operating theatre. Everything, including my hands, was covered with splashes of red. It was all worth it, though: at the end of the meal Yura kissed me three times (which he says is the traditional way to say thank you) and said, 'That meal was normal,' in a happy voice. He meant it was exactly like the *borscht* he had at home.

Good morning, Janice

The wind is whipping through the garden like a whirling dervish, screaming as it passes. Very soon Harry is going to grab me by my Swanndri hoodie and drag me out to muster the ewes down from Milo. We will draft the Corriedale rams out and draft some Oxford rams in. The ewes will then head for Mt Lance via Tommy's Creek, and then we go out for drinks. It is Friday. We are going to meet a dairy farmer friend who used to be a sheep farmer for dinner at the Hurunui pub. If he looks smug, I will hit him. Dairy farmers are floating in milk solids, dollars and glee. Sheep farmers are drowning in debt and sorrow.

The cows who passed all their tests, TB and pregnancy, are returning to the winter hills. Yesterday my old dogs and I drove the main herd out into a painted afternoon, the blue, pale sky empty in its bowl of hills, and the land flat against the light; not a bird sang and the creek was so low it slunk silently between the banks. To walk into a painted afternoon is to discover stillness, silence and total aloneness. You would not want to be an agoraphobic, you would find menace in the empty sky and terror in the silent hills. I am not agoraphobic, I love painted afternoons. The cows sloped sullenly along, neither glad nor sad to be leaving the paddocks behind them. They are headed for Rollet's Gully. When I shut the gate behind the last cow, Toby crept up to my knee for a pat. He is old and I wonder whether he will do another weaning muster. Sometimes I wonder, will I? It's hard on bones and joints, and my nerve is a bit gone after being charged by a very wild cow last year. It is no fun wearing a cow's head in your chest.

You will be pleased to learn that Janice (the cow) was not subjected to the indignity of a probe in her rectum to determine pregnancy. She and Doris sat in the horse paddock and watched proceedings from afar. Janice and Doris do not mix with ordinary cows — and Janice will surely be in calf, I told Harry.

Here's Harry, it's ten o'clock, maybe he can be tempted to coffee before we leave.

(Yes, he was tempted.) What a day: coffee and drinks — what you city slickers do all the time.

Dear Virginia

The nearest I come to mustering in freezing weather is taking a bunch of Irish rugby fanatics to the Cake Tin for the Irish test. I am not looking forward to it because they don't believe me when I say the weather will turn cold and wet tonight and they must dress up well. They won't hear of covering their green shirts with coats and hats. I fear the in-coming southerly.

Dear Janice

You will be sitting in the Cake Tin waiting for the game to start. We cannot watch because our Sky dish is full of snow. There is no signal; it would be foolish and dangerous to cling onto the roof and sweep the dish clean, and who cares whether we win or lose anyway. I have just walked down to the shearers' quarters to turn on the lights for a pig-shooter who is coming in later tonight to, hopefully, shoot a boar for the Parnassus pig-shooting competition in the morning. As I walked back up the paddock and cast my torchlight into the snow-covered pine trees, I thought: if you lived in a city you would never, ever walk a snowy paddock alone in the dark, you would never look into a black sky and see the snow catch the torchlight as it falls. There is always light in a city, and rapists and squeezers and other mean and ugly people. You would never hear the silence of snow.

Dear Virginia

There is no silence in this household at the moment. The reason for this is the Irish. When the Irish come to stay, I never get a moment to do anything except eat, drink, talk, and drink some more. The weekend started for me early on Friday morning with cleaning up after the Russian night, then caramelizing cups of onions to make yet more *pissaladière* as snacks for the Irish. You can cheat by using a pizza base from the supermarket. It's great to spend time and effort cross-hatching anchovies all over the top of the onions. It's that city thing again: it looks as though it took ages to make, but actually it's easy to muster anchovies into a pattern. I can do either weaving patterns with them or sun-burst patterns, and I was never good at crafts, even at playschool. The sweet and salty in this tart is great together, especially when you're drinking. And the effort is noticed.

For dinner tonight I had California David, the drama director, meeting Porirua David the sound engineer. Their common ground was the learning of Spanish. The Irish arrived just as we were sitting down to eat. I knew it would be like feeding the 5,000 this weekend, so I'd made a huge pot of *dahl*, with *naan* bread and rice. Everyone was fed. After their stomachs were nicely lined, the Irish went into town — about 11pm. They fell through the door again at 3am and were up again by ten.

'Oh no, no, Janice, no breakfast, thank you so very much. We'll have it in town. It's a Gaelic football fundraiser: $20 for breakfast — two slices of toast and two pints of Guinness.'

I put away the eggs and the omelette pan.

Off they went, California David in tow for the cultural experience.

'It's going to rain,' I said, 'and turn very cold.'

'Oh, no, no, no, Janice,' they said.

We joined them in the afternoon for a spot of drinking and a lot of talking over an Irish band and over most of the Irish expats in New Zealand who were all shouting 'Where you from?' at each other. California David was nowhere to be seen.

When I returned home, California David was lying down, recovering from the 'breakfast'. We got kitted out. As Robert was in Canada, he'd got his flatmate in Auckland to send me his precious AB jersey for me to wear. David said he had Irish ancestry and produced a (brand-new) Irish shirt. At 7pm the real Irish returned from drinking breakfast to join a group of us who were impatiently waiting for them. I repeated what I'd been saying all day: take rain gear and lots of wool.

'Oh, no, no, Janice. That won't be necessary.'

We walked to the Cake Tin: the stumbling Irish, California David — recovered from one cultural experience and ready for the next one — and me with a large bag of woolly hats, scarves, gloves, even over-trousers. Still no one believed me when I said we had to be prepared for the southerly and rain.

As we climbed the steps away from the humdrum and into the magical, onto that triumphant walkway that arches high across the railway yards and carries 30,000 people up through the darkness to the brightly lit curve of the Cake Tin, our hearts lightened, and — then the rain fell. Like shrapnel. I had only one cycle cape and one pair of over-trousers in my life-support bag. I needed 10 of each. Most of us were going to be soaked.

Our seats were two rows from the front — to get up close and be part of things, said Gerald. They were also wet. California David disappeared. We didn't know where. I tried to share my cycle cape with Gerald, but it only went so far. Dan had had open-heart surgery six weeks before. Tony looked quite frail, but that could have been the all-day 'breakfast'. A couple of hours, sitting, saturated, in a pool of water, in a freezing southerly could finish them off completely, which wasn't quite what 'beating the Irish' was meant to mean.

It's not what you know but who you know . . . With quick texting before the fingers became uncontrollable with cold, Olive managed to get access to a corporate box, with huge, round tables covered in fine linen and elaborate food, and warm people in suits or light cashmere jerseys. I never knew people went to games wearing suits! We shed piles of sodden woolly clothing and jackets, scarves, hats, gloves, and the cycle cape of course. We mounded them into a compost-like heap that steamed in a corner by the coffee/tea table. We headed for the bar. Then we bypassed all the big, round dining tables of bored business people, and carried our tray out to the balcony. We were at one end of the field, not on the halfway line where we like to sit, but we weren't complaining. We spent the game drinking hot-water whiskies and beers. Afterwards, when we were partying on in the corporate box which everyone else had deserted, I noticed I was still wearing my over-trousers.

Hello, Janice

I know you can cope with Irishmen coming to stay, but they are probably easy to entertain because you can just shove them out the door and tell them to go to a pub where they will be perfectly happy drinking Guinness. I want to tell you about having farmers to visit, and to prepare you in case any do turn up on your doorstep. It is bull-sale time, a time when farmers are on the move and inclined to drop in. I will illustrate how to cater for farmers by telling you about a visit we made to city friends after a bull sale.

The bull sale was out at Lincoln, so we had to skirt around Christchurch to get there. On the way home we decided to drive in to the city and visit Brian and Gill. We expected to find Brian lying pale and ill on a couch because he is having chemotherapy, but he was out. We drank a glass of wine with Gill while we waited. When Brian eventually materialized, he looked extremely bouncy and healthy and suggested we open another bottle of wine. Harry and I had not formulated an exit plan because we thought we were visiting an invalid who would be very tired and would not want to drink wine. Harry did not see my 'it's time to go' look; we sat on, drinking wine. Suddenly it was nine o'clock. 'Ah,' says Brian, 'we can't let you go home without eating. Gill will cook up something, won't you, Gill? Another glass of wine, Harry?' Gill looks absolutely thrilled at having to conjure a scratch meal for a couple of farmers who don't have an exit plan. Harry and Brian have another glass of wine. Gill throws together an admirable meal from things she has in the deep-freeze. This is what you will need for an impromptu farmer tea.

Desperate Hostess Designer Burgers

Ciabatta buns, minced venison, an avocado, some tomatoes, lettuce, Gruyère cheese, tomato relish, mayonnaise and sour cream.

This is what you do. Defrost the mince and the buns. Form the mince into patties and sear in a little oil. Split the buns in half and toast under the grill with the Gruyère cheese on half of them. Put the buns on a plate. On the buns with the cheese, spread a lettuce leaf, sliced avocado and tomato and garnish with sour cream and mayonnaise.

On the other half-bun spread a lick of tomato relish, and on top of this place a venison patty. Grind lots of pepper over the patty, and decorate the plate with a few artful slices of tomato and avocado.

Serve to the farmers, who will eat it all up with gusto and then go home if you give them a strong coffee to ensure they wake up enough to drive the car.

You must now go out and lay in supplies for the bull-sale season in case of farmers' visits. If the farmers do not arrive, you can feed the designer venison burgers to the Irish.

Dear Virginia

I have never thawed something in the microwave. Think of the carbon footprint! In fact, I never use a microwave. And the Irish don't want venison. They like Irish stew — simple slow-cooking of stewing steak, onions and potatoes. Get meat with plenty of gristle and tendons in it — it's more delicious. And don't brown the onions.

Dear Janice

It is tragic, but city people see feeding farmers only in terms of meat, so when we arrive unexpectedly they think 'meat, must have meat', when really we would be quite happy with an egg, or *hummus* for that matter. We do 'do' vegetables. But the burgers did look very arty, and I'm sure the carbon footprint of the microwave was less than driving down to the takeaway or eating out at a little café.

I am not normally inside sitting at the computer at ten in the morning, but I am making cheese and I have to wait 45 minutes for the rennet to set the curd, and after that I have to cut the curd and then let it pitch for 5 minutes, and then I have to heat it again and pitch it and cheddar it and press it. It is Thursday; I should be making cheeses on Saturday. Two years ago I went on a cheese-making course with New Zealand's leading home cheese-making tutor, a hugely enthusiastic woman called Katherine Mowbray — she is so thin she doesn't look as though she would eat cheese, but she does. I caught her enthusiasm for cheese-making with the ease with which you pick up a cold in winter, and I bought all the paraphernalia, press, culture, buckets, muslin, cheese cloth, a thermometer, a new very huge saucepan. (Do not ask how much all this cost.) And then I didn't make any cheese.

Cheese-making has become a synonym for procrastination at Double Tops — 'must go and make the cheese'. Last Saturday, Dugald next door decided it was time to put an end to putting off the cheese. He milks a cow every morning; he told me very firmly that he would shut the calves out for a night during the week — this increases the milk supply. Last night he rang, 'The milk will be ready for you at 8.30 tomorrow morning.' I couldn't weasel out of cheese-making any more.

And here I am ready to go and cut the curd . . .

. . . Good evening, I cut the curd and then very slowly lifted the temperature to 38 degrees, and all the while stirred it gently with my hands to break the curd and squeeze the moisture out; this took 35 minutes. Then I ladled off the whey and tipped the curd out onto a muslin-covered rack. I cheddared the curd; this took a long time and is too complicated to explain. After the cheddaring I had to mill the cheese, which means to break the curd into walnut-sized lumps, then it had to be salted and after that wrapped in muslin and pressed into a mould. After the moulding I put the mould onto the press and screwed the pressure screws, and by that time it was one o'clock and I was almost deranged. As well as the huge quantities of time, there were stringent hygiene requirements, and I had turned into an obsessive/compulsive lunatic engaged in elaborate hand-washing and utensil-rinsing rituals.

I let the cheese out of the press after 15 minutes and turned it over. The 5 litres of milk had yielded 500g of white, bouncy, elastic-looking lumps of curd, and I rang Dugald and told him he could stick his milk and his cows, and I went out to work in my broom swamp which I'm restoring to a native swamp. I spent the afternoon hacking out giant broom bushes and piling them into windrows for burning. When I came back inside at six, I released the pressure on the press and unmoulded the 500g of cheese so I could turn it over again; the white, bouncy, elastic disc had morphed into a pale yellow disc of cheese. It was the most beautiful cheese I've ever seen. Good things take time. I rang Dugald and told him I would need more milk — in time.

I re-wrapped the disc and put it back in the press bottom-side up, where it will stay until the morning when it has to be soaked in a 20% brine solution for 2 hours, after that it has to be stored somewhere. I will store it in some sort of contraption in the pantry. The pantry has a slatted window to the south; it is very cold, a little like a cave. Every 2 or 3 days I will go into the cheese cave and brine-wash the cheese to inhibit mould growing on the rind. Good cheese doesn't take time, it takes eras. I have no idea when it will be ready to eat, maybe I will frame it instead.

I should buy a cheese-drying cupboard to hang in the pantry, but cheese-making expenses have already run into hundreds and hundreds of dollars, so ingenuity is called for. As I made the cheese I thought about all the farmers who have made cheese for thousands of years. They didn't know about hygiene, and they didn't need thermometers and two huge stainless-steel saucepans sitting one inside the other, and sterilized muslin and sanitizing tablets and racks and plastic dishes and stainless steel ladles and spoons and a fancy cheese press. (Neither did I, but the little blue pottery press was a very seductive item of equipment.)

Every farmer's wife probably made cheese in a dirty old dairy, and she probably used pottery bowls and crocks and tested the temperature by the heat of the milk on her hand and weighted the press with bricks, and every now and then people probably became ill from a bad cheese, but back then no one would have had to register the illness with the medical officer of health, so no one else would have become alarmed unless the town crier called the news around town, and there were probably more important things to cry about.

Dear Virginia

I have never made cheese. I leave that up to the old guys at Mainland.

Last night, when most people I know were watching the rugby test, against the English this time, I went to Rachel's pantry evening. We had, as instructed, each brought a dish representing our cultural heritage and multiple copies of the recipe used. The recipes were to ensure that anyone with allergies or food taboos could check that no forbidden food was contained in the concoctions. I'd made a Shortest-Day Cake, a culturally-inclusive version of a Christmas cake.

The pantry door was flung wide and the pantry glowed as the light from its own overhead bulb — not an energy-saving one, I noticed — sparkled off the shiny surfaces of four shelves full of stainless-steel and glass canisters, all labelled. And what labels! I was speechless. There were star anise, cardamoms, fenugreek seeds, an aphrodisiacal Tibetan tea given to Rachel by Tibetan monks. An Indian mouth-freshener called *mukwhas*, looking like tiny sprinkles of purple, red and silver, was passed round for us all to dab at and taste. There was black rice which turns purple when you cook it and is great for desserts. Every sort of bean and seed.

There was *quinoa* grain and *quinoa* flour. One guest said *quinoa* was from Ancient Egypt. Another said, Excuse me, no, it was from the ancient Incas. I didn't ask about its use-by date. There was seaweed from Korean shops, soy flour, *miso* paste. And oils, vinegars and baking soda — more about baking soda later. There was even a glass jar of ground eggshells. That's what the label said. I asked what they were for.

The ground eggshells are a source of calcium if you don't eat eggs. You procure the eggshells — free range, organic —

from someone who doesn't want to put them in her compost (I didn't ask why you wouldn't want to put eggshells in your compost). You grind them up and put them into a glass with lemon juice. It froths up as the calcium is freed from the shells, and you drink it. (You see, Virginia, yet another way to eat calcium, equal in complexity to your cheese-making. Am I the only person who just goes to the supermarket and buys a brick of Mainland cheddar? Is it cheating?)

We gathered in the middle of the kitchen, beside the glowing pantry, for a blessing before the meal began. We drank a toast of Rejuvelac juice (sprouted wheat). I realized, then, that it was going to be an alcohol-free evening. After we'd eaten, we talked about food, and sometimes the food talk morphed into housework talk. The most ardent debate was about baking soda.

Baking soda is so great to clean with that you don't need anything else at all. Clean yourself, clean your clothes, clean the bath, clean the windows, clean the car engine.

'I was doing my feet in the shower,' confessed a chatty woman. 'I was pumice-ing them and using soda, as you do. The glass wall of the stall was dirty so I just soda-ed that too. Worked brilliantly. Clean feet. Clean shower.'

'And it cures cancer,' said Louise, who told us that you boil baking soda with maple syrup, and eat a spoonful of that a day. The maple syrup acts as a conductor to get the baking soda into your cells. Without the maple syrup it would only go to your stomach. 'And when it's in the cells it is alkaline,' she said triumphantly. 'And' — pause for effect — 'cancer cells are acid, so they're gone. Just like that.'

'But why doesn't anyone know about this?' asked a young, newly married woman.

'Because there's no money in baking soda.'

We all sighed. The world is so tricky.

Then a Steiner mum asked: 'What *is* baking soda?'

'It's a rock, I think,' said the show-off chef who had been talking only moments before about trans-fats' molecular changes when heated.

'Can you get organic baking soda?' asked the Steiner mum.

'Can rocks be organic?' asked the artist.

The conversation paused, then the German *frau* announced that baking soda was a good enema. The room suddenly divided, as though cut by a knife, into those who believed in enemas and those who hadn't tried it. Those who hadn't tried it identified themselves by shrieking with laughter.

'Did Princess Di use baking soda? You know, with her colonic irrigation?' one of two sisters asked.

'It makes your skin real smooth,' someone else said, 'so she probably did.'

Into the serious contemplation that now descended like a candle-snuffer in the wind, the cheerful German *frau* said, 'And it's good for cleaning little boy's peckers. Stops them getting infections.'

'What is?' asked a confused, older woman.

'She had two of them, after all,' said a photographer.

'Who? Diana?'

'Two whats?' asked the Indian lawyer.

One woman, who had a head cold, wanted to know if you could snort baking soda.

'For my cold,' she said, sneezing into the green salad no one had eaten.

'It's too harsh for the nose,' someone said.

'But if you use it in an enema . . .'

'Not us. We don't. Just Germans.'

The Indian woman told us about *waggar*, which is the

process of popping seeds — mustard, fenugreek, cumin etc — before adding them to the curry spices. We learnt how to mop up food the Indian way, elegantly, with three fingers. We all smelt a pot of *asafoetida* which was passed around the circle. One culturally insensitive woman said it smelt like Rotorua. 'Ugh.' She shuddered. When the woman with the cold breathed in the asafoetida she sneezed into the pot.

Dessert. I noticed one show-off chef had written the nutritional profile per truffle on her recipe sheet for carob and raisin truffles. There were big figs, too. I said I wanted to dip my fig in brandy and everyone laughed. My cake wasn't acceptable to most people. It had eggs in it — horrors! And wheat flour — horrors! Sugar — horrors! *And* 200 grams of finest NZ butter. Beyond horror. But it was a divine cake; very, very rich. I really craved a whisky now.

The just-married woman and I took the train home. The train was full of people already too drunk to drive or excitedly planning to get that way. As the train pulled into her station, a figure was running along the road to the platform. She giggled 'That's my husband', and slipped out into the night with her bag of samples of the night's dishes — *dahl*, salads, and a big slab of cake.

Dear Janice

Oh dear!! I can cope with composters, dairy allergies, vegans, bean sprouters, baking soda cleaners and lentil munchers, in fact I'm rather partial to lentils myself; but I am hopelessly suspicious of people who don't drink wine — unless they are members of the AA. This suspicion, which is deeply politically incorrect, was fostered by my father who called all non-drinkers wowsers. I know alcohol strangles brain cells, but Rejuvelac juice sounds very disgusting. If I had been at the pantry party I would have been, like you, dreaming of a whisky with the decadent fruit cake.

I must try cleaning the shower with baking soda. It cleans the inside of the teapot like a miracle cleaner. If you move to baking soda cleaning, buy it at a swimming-pool shop where you can buy it in bulk for a fraction of the supermarket price. It is sold as a pH-increase product. I don't believe in enemas; when I worked at the Cornwall geriatric hospital as a student, patients were sent off for colonic irrigation on a regular basis. They were terrified of 'colonic' and dreaded it as much as I remembered dreading the call to the Murder House to have my teeth drilled by the murderesses with the foot-powered dental drill.

Dear Virginia

At work, the CEO has just ordered 150 chocolate fish to take to New Jersey to woo sales reps. It's odd to think that chocolate fish represent New Zealand cuisine.

July

Dear Janice

Today is the first of July. Winter begins. The swimming pool has frozen over. Thankfully Alvin is not in it. Alvin is the little aqua-bug bottom-cleaner and last year he got frozen in for a whole month; it was not a good look.

I have had the wood range in the kitchen going for a couple of weeks now. It has a huge appetite for wood, and I feel beholden to it — beholden to keep feeding it, and beholden to it for the benefits it brings to the kitchen. When the Wellstood is burning it makes sense to cook meals that need long, slow cooking. I will use local ingredients: root vegetables from the garden and no out-of-season imports. However, I have to point out the folly of being anti-imports. As farmers we survive on out-of-season exporting, so we cannot afford to adopt an insular attitude to imported food and yet still expect other countries to buy our lamb.

I will make bone soup. This is a terrible name for a soup, but it came from Mrs Ewart and the name has stuck. Bone soup is made from bones, beef or mutton, boiled for a very long time to make a meaty broth to which you add vegetables of all kinds. You do remove the bones, as the soup looks primeval if you leave them in. I add grated onion, potato, carrots, pumpkin, split peas and lentils. I make the soup in a huge stockpot, and one brew does a whole week of lunches. The flavour improves and the broth thickens by the day, and you can add leftovers to the pot if you think they will enhance the flavour.

Tonight I cooked lentils instead of potatoes to serve with the lamb chops. Not just any lentils: Puy lentils served in a rich tomato-and-herb sauce. You would have thought the apocalypse was nigh. Harry was devastated. What! No potatoes? Total ruin of a good lamb chop . . . He went on and on. Two of our friends who are avid lentil-eaters have heart problems, therefore lentils equal heart disease. Harry's eloquence on the evils of lentils was countered by Fleur pointing out that he had spooned a second helping onto his plate, whereupon he said that he was starving and that you need twice as many lentils as you need potatoes to fill the gap.

Harry is a meat-and-potatoes man, but, poor man, he is married to me and has to submit to having his food seriously interfered with. He is mostly very tolerant, but lentils bring him to a point just a tad below boiling. To follow the lentils I made him an apple crumble with the last of the roadside apples, and that mollified him a little.

Fleur is living at home for a month, which is a treat. She is a wonderful sheep dog, and we have made good use of her mountain-running skills over the last two weeks. In between musters she runs great loops round the farm tracks, and cycles to the end of the road and back again, and helps shift breaks, and bakes Harry chocolate-chip biscuits which warms his heart. I do not have time to cook chocolate-chip biscuits.

I would very much like your recipe for pumpkin and coconut cream soup which you describe as an iconic New Zealand soup and which I have never made or tasted. I want to make it while Fleur is here. I would also like your Christmas cake recipe.

Dear Virginia

Here is the recipe. It is a common soup in Wellington cafés in winter.

Pumpkin and Coconut Cream Soup

½ a large pumpkin

1 tbsp oil or butter

1 large onion, sliced

2 green chillies, deseeded and chopped

1 nail-sized piece of ginger, diced (I am generous
   with the ginger)

2 cloves garlic

1½ litres stock

salt and pepper

1 tin coconut cream (The Samoa brand is the one to get.
   I say why buy Thai when you can support the Islands?
   And it is very creamy and delicious)

fresh coriander or mint

Dice and peel pumpkin and discard seeds, etc. Cook onion, chillies, ginger, garlic in oil until translucent. Add diced pumpkin and cover in stock. Simmer half an hour (approx) until tender.

Blend, purée or just mash so the soup is smooth. Reheat with salt and pepper and coconut cream. Serve hot with fresh coriander on top.

I am sorry Harry doesn't like lentils. I know what he means. Potatoes are by far the most satisfying, and the most versatile, of the starches. I am not a rice-eater. I can't understand why anyone would want rice when they could have potatoes. But lentils — I love *dahl*, so I eat them fairly often. They are useful when chaotic visitors arrive from out of town for the weekend and you're not sure if you'll be eating in or out.

This week, most of the time the atmosphere at work was calm, almost stodgy, like gravy that has thickened too much. The stodginess was caused by too many meetings. To give you an idea of what a meeting is like, here's what happened in this morning's one. The tallest person was chosen to be the chairperson. We had to line up to decide who this was. Then we sat down and stared at the whiteboard.

'Shall I be scribe?' Emily finally asked.

Someone said, 'Let's get our thinking into circles.' Emily drew circles on the board, concentric circles like those in a pond after a penny has dropped. But no penny dropped.

Someone else said, 'Now we can marry up what we're doing in clusters with our five-year vision.'

'We must factor in the resources to support the developments,' droned someone else.

Emily scribed away.

'Could I chime in with the fact there is some project slippage?' asked someone else.

I tried to slip away when they were all so deep in slippage-thought I was sure they wouldn't notice my leaving.

But, alas: 'Janice, we want to capture some of your thinking before you go.'

I enjoy the humour of the office, the gallows humour of people all trapped together. I also enjoy the teamwork and the professional challenges. We are all proud of what we produce together. (Help me! I nearly said, 'at the end of the day'.) But there are other things now that I think I could enjoy more. I blame your letters, Virginia. Your blasts of fresh air are changing my 'thinking' and my 'vision'. Maybe there is another way of living, even if I don't grind my roasted coriander seeds, know how to fire up a wood range, and don't want to make cheese?

I can't imagine Harry in the office for one second. I don't like to think how he would cope if he received these instructions on how to get out of a lift, but then I guess there are few lifts in the Hawarden back country: *Tena koutou. The lifts are levelling to our floor level randomly today so please take care and LOOK DOWN when walking into/out of the lifts! H & S regulations apply. Ka kite.*

That was, of course, from Human Resources. HR had a good week. One of them left an astonishing note for one of the male editors: *Kick down my door and talk to me about briefs.*

When I came home from work, Ron (of the potato garden further up the terrace) was working in his small glass-house. Would you like a glass-house in your garden? If I had room, I would. His is full of chillies at the moment. Hundreds of them. I took a large bag of them home. They are very festive and delicious, and they look like Christmas-tree lights. I spent the evening doing desperation snacking, thinking of the pros and cons of leaving work, eating hard licorice and a block of Whittaker's Dark Orange.

I must now make some pastry cases for tomorrow's FEDs.

Good afternoon, Janice

My retirement dream, after we leave the farm and these cold hills, is to live in a place where I can grow tomatoes. Harry says, 'Well that's easy. You don't need to leave the farm to grow tomatoes. You just need a glass-house.' So, I have mixed feelings about a glass-house. It might delay retirement forever.

On the other hand, a little glass-house is a thing I've coveted all my life.

Batten down the windows, secure the doors! There's bad weather coming. It's snowing and blowing in the hills and the air temperature is 1 degree. It'll be a rough night at the Cake Tin for the visiting Springboks. Are you going down there to watch the game, or are you watching it on a big screen from the safety of a pub bar? Mandy and Dugald are coming to watch on our small, old-fashioned TV set which is quite adequate for people like us who watch very little TV. I do not know who any of the Springboks are, but once I've had that glass of wine it won't matter.

I didn't make the pumpkin soup for lunch today because I couldn't be bothered with all that mashing and stuff. I made a hearty soup called Galician Broth which I found in a Spanish cook-book. I didn't follow the recipe exactly, because I didn't have quite all the ingredients.

Galician Broth

The recipe called for a 500g piece of gammon; I used 500g of bacon ends. I always have a vacuum-pack of bacon ends in the fridge. They are very useful for emergencies. I put the chopped bacon ends in 1½ litres of water along with 2 sliced onions and 3 bay leaves from the garden. I boiled the bacon and onions for about 20 minutes, and then I added 2 tsp paprika (not smoked paprika — I think it smells just like Stockholm tar which we paint on horses' hooves and it makes me feel like throwing up) and 500g of potatoes chopped into chunks, plus a can of *cannellini* beans and ground black pepper. I boiled the soup until it had reduced and thickened. The recipe said to add spring greens right at the last minute, but it was snowing by then and I didn't want to go out into the garden again to pick silverbeet, which would have been a substitute for spring greens. Next time I make it I think I will use Lima beans because they make themselves more noticeable than *cannellini* beans do.

PS: What are FEDs?

Hello, Virginia

FEDs are Friday evening drinks.

It is cold. The wind is howling around the house. The ferries aren't running. The airport will be like the Gobi Desert on a bad day. But there is a bit of sun coming into the house. Jane and I will meet up for our Sunday afternoon walk, regardless of weather.

Last night I didn't watch the ABs. Family is stronger than AB-watching, and Tanya (niece) and Garry invited me for dinner last night. They are artists, and they live in a world in which no AB plays a part. I don't think they knew the game was on. Thank goodness New Zealand now supports a sufficiently diverse population that not everyone has to do the same thing on AB test night. I received an email with a 'Go the ABs' message from Robert in the Arctic just before I set off to Seatoun where T and G have a flat.

I brought course number one: we ate guacamole (lots of NZ avocados in the supermarket at the moment) with whole-wheat Bordeaux French bread, and wine. Tanya made stuffed *cannelloni*, baked in a tomato sauce and topped with grated cheese. Then we had ice cream with blueberries — the last of those from the Taumarunui blueberry farm I've mentioned before. A very good winter feast.

Garry told me about the whale's heart (life-sized) that he'd made for Te Papa's whale exhibit. The first one didn't last the rigours of thousands of children crawling through it, and was now on a farm out of Palmerston North. The second one, a successfully tough-enough one, is travelling the world with the exhibition. He's now making fake translucent alabaster vessels that are supposed to be 2,000 years old, for some god-bothering company to send to potential investors to promote the *Kingdom Come* film that's about to be filmed in the South Island. We laughed about that. I don't associate Jesus with snowy scenery, do you?

Tanya showed me the material for her wedding dress which her clever mother is making. She showed me her entries for this year's Wearable Arts — a wooden dress in the architecture section, based on extraordinary buildings in New Caledonia, and a takahe dress, complete with big knobbly red feet. The wedding dress, I should say quickly, is silk and more conventional.

We spent the rest of the evening around their wood burner — burning old timber from an Indian church in Newtown that's being renovated by a builder friend of theirs who came around for the evening to share the wood's warmth.

Friday night, 4th of July, I went to a family dinner hosted and cooked by Becqui, my American/Lebanese sister-in-law. We had the total works — the huge turkey, and the apple pie that was about 6 inches deep. Hugh and Becqui have been in Singapore for some years and have recently returned with their Fijian-, Singaporean- and American-educated children. So the feast was special, because it is years since we all enjoyed the Becqui version of 4 July.

Here's the cake recipe I forgot to send before. I love making fruit cake in mid-winter. It is quick and so easy. I always take one up to Bill's.

Christmas Cake (or Shortest Day Cake)

Day 1

Soak 1kg of mixed dried fruit in ½ cup of liquid — either sherry, rum or tea. I always add prunes for a rich, dark colour.

Day 2

In a big bowl, rub 200g butter into 2 cups flour. Add ½ cup sugar, ½ tsp baking soda, and salt. Add the dried fruit.

In another bowl, mix 2 eggs, ½ cup milk, ¼ cup honey. Add this to main mixture. Stir (with hands).

Put into 1 large or 2 small cake tins. Bake at 160 degrees Celsius for 2½ hours.

I did hear recently that some people don't like rubbing butter into flour, and hence don't make scones and pastry because they don't like getting butter under their fingernails. I don't know what to say about this other than to advise them to wash their hands. Imagine a life lived without getting your hands dirty!

Keep warm!

Hello, Janice

I hate July. It is such a cold, capricious month, but maybe you don't notice this in Thorndon where your garden doesn't freeze solid and the yard doesn't turn to mud. July is not a good month for visitors, but last Thursday we entertained visitors from Aberdeen and South Korea; they were Sinclair relatives, all part of the reverse diaspora. A hundred-and-fifty years ago the clan fled the highlands of Scotland. Now they are fleeing New Zealand. They stayed at Double Tops for one freezing-cold night. We gave them a hill-country time. A shot of whisky beside the fire before tea, roast hogget pocked with garlic and scattered with rosemary slow-roasted in the wood range, baked pumpkin, herb-roasted Agria potatoes, parsnip crisps, and slightly steamed, buttered broccoli. For pudding I made a Boongy which we ate with ice cream and cream.

Boongy is the name Kit and Fleur gave to a hot pudding I used to make for the shearers when we shore with the blades and the shearers stayed for days on end in the shearers' quarters. Boongy is a variation on Dominion pudding which you can find in the Edmonds cook-book. It is a very easy-to-make, unsophisticated pudding, but it is the sort of pudding you feel like eating in the depths of winter. You always eat too much of it, and too much makes you feel boongied up, hence the name Boongy.

Boongy

150g butter

1 cup sugar

3 eggs

2 cups flour

3 tsp baking powder

½ cup milk

2 tsp vanilla

½ cup golden syrup

Cream butter and sugar, beat in the eggs. Add the sifted flour and baking powder alternately with the milk and vanilla.

Grease a 2-litre bowl, put the golden syrup in the bottom and then spoon the pudding mixture on top. Cover the bowl with baking paper and secure with a thick rubber band. Put the bowl into a saucepan of water, put the lid on and steam the pudding for 1½ hours. If you are not sure whether it is done, cook some more. You cannot over-cook a boongy unless you let the pot boil dry.

Turn the boongy out on a plate and serve with ice cream. The Edmonds book says serve with custard, but I don't think so. This recipe makes a big pudding, enough for a shearing gang. I would halve it if you are making it for a city crowd.

We drank two bottles of Merlot with the hogget. Is Merlot right with hogget? I don't know. Must email wine expert John Hawkesby — he would probably recommend a wine 'with a hint of caramel and blackcurrant overlaid with tea leaves and an after-taste of black turnip' that would be a mere snip at $50.

I must also tell you about the parsnip crisps. The despised parsnip has been elevated to a delicacy vegetable. I'm besotted with parsnip crisps. Do this.

Parsnip Crisps

Dig a few parsnips from the garden, wash and peel. Then, take one of those wide Swiss vegetable peelers and shave slices of parsnip until there is so little parsnip left you are in danger of slicing your fingers. (I'm sure a mandolin would be better, but I don't have one.) Heat some oil in a pan — quite hot — and fry the parsnip shavings until crisp and curly golden. They look exotic, they taste divine, and they go with almost anything.

Most springs I dig all the knotty old parsnips out and throw them on the compost heap; this winter I don't think I will have enough parsnips.

After breakfast — breakfast for the guests, morning coffee for us — we drove out in the Toyota to muster the ewes off Tricky Spur. Never have we had so many English-speaking dogs at our disposal. Harry sent them off in all directions.

Dear Virginia

That sounds like a great weekend! My entertaining was less well planned. The weekend started with the typical FEDs — Friday evening drinks. Owen arrived unexpectedly to cheer himself up after a week of mustering computers. He is one of my oldest friends here. We worked together at Capital Radio in London years ago.

Drinks after work, whatever the day of the week, are a fatal institution. You often haven't eaten since breakfast — a banana and a coffee — and suddenly you are chugging back the Sauvignon Blanc and telling all sorts of stories on an empty stomach. So I've learnt the hard way how to prepare for this dangerous occasion. You always have some sort of snack-making ingredients you can just chuck in the blender or mash, or plonk on a plate, to go with the wine. AND you always have a defrosted jar of very nourishing soup to eat after you've waved them all goodbye so you can sober up.

Lurking unloved in the fridge, I had two leftover potatoes from last night. I mashed them with butter, opened a tin of mackerel and mashed it all together. I galloped down the garden path to wrench a lemon from the tree, and some rocket from the garden. I added the lemon juice to the mash, added lots of pepper because I didn't have time to chop chillies. I pasted the fish mash onto slabs of French bread, added the rocket artistically to the top of each one, and arranged them on a large plate in concentric circles. I also made pea-and-mint dip which is so simple — mash up peas and mint with grated Parmesan.

8.30, the food had all gone, as had several bottles of something white and wet. After the visitors had gone into the dark, wet night, we had coconut cream and pumpkin soup. It's divine and it's sobering. I felt boongied.

Last week's FEDs were better planned: I grilled the peppers for *rouillé* the night before.

Rouillé

Grill 2 red peppers over the gas flame. (I couldn't cook without gas. That would be a problem in the country.) Put the blackened peppers in a paper bag for a while, then rub off their skins. Purée the cooked peppers with 2 cloves of garlic and a thick slice of bread you've soaked in water then squeezed. (Designer breads go stale very quickly, so this is a useful way of using stale bread.) Pour into the blender ½ cup of olive oil. Do this slowly, like you would for mayo. Serve on crackers.

Dear Janice

It is a long time since I went to Friday evening drinks; I remember the last time well. It was a Friday in the February of 1974. Friends and I walked over the road to the Gonorrhoea, which is what all the hospital staff called the pub across the road. Not because it was the sort of place you might encounter a venereal disease, but because it had once been a nice, comfortable old pub called the Royal and a smart developer bought it, tarted it up and called it the Grenadier. It had war memorabilia on the walls, which were fortified with large pictures of Grenadier Guards. It was no longer a nice, comfortable old place to drink, and so it gradually became known, amongst hospital staff, as the Gonorrhoea. I left the hospital at the end of February, and on the first of March Harry and I drove up to Double Tops to begin our farming career. I never went out to Friday evening drinks again.

How I miss that Friday night feeling, the seam that delineates work from weekend. How I miss the concept of weekend. Our weeks are often seamless. Harry doesn't do weekends unless it is the hunting season or unless I drag him off to the city, which he tolerates — just. The minute we arrive he is ready to depart for the hills. Cities hold no thrall for him and the coffee is always too cold.

Dear Virginia

Maybe he'd like Gotham in Chews Lane. They really try to bring you very hot coffee if you ask for it. Don't get carried away by the fun of FEDs and a weekend in which to recover. Remember that in order to have these things you have to have an office job Monday to Friday.

Office life isn't all bad. There's something heroic about it, too. The discipline, the politeness, the cooperation. An upside is the childish, semi-hysterical humour that easily erupts from nothing. For example, an editor received an email from IT saying: *Your program has shipped with ADB port dongles. The dongles should have been for the USB port.* The editor replied: *Sorry to hear of your unfortunate circumstances with the wrong dongles. I hope the condition is treatable.* These two emails got the 'All Staff' distribution, so everyone joined in. Rupert put a card at Reception for people to sign: *For John, who is experiencing trouble with his dongles.* John replied: *The rumour that I'm experiencing trouble with my dongles is untrue. They are in perfect working order. Just the wrong shape.*

Teams had personality-testing workshops last week. The average personality type for our team was Extrovert, Intuitive, Feeling, Judging type of person. The only person who had all those qualities was Rupert. Ergo — Rupert is the radiant embodiment of the team. A cult is developing. I've advised everyone not to give him money.

I have been doing market research into chocolate fish. The little dairy below the office building sells 300 chocolate fish a week. These are used as incentives at team meetings. There are many public servants and government departments around here.

Dear Janice

Chocolate fish sound very juvenile as a reward. I used them as mustering incentives when Kit and Fleur had short legs and small minds.

I could not work in an office: today I sat all day at my computer and I ate twice as much food and drank three times as much coffee as I usually do. I would be obese if I were an office person. At four o'clock my head was all done in, so I put on all my wet-weather gear and took the dogs walking for an hour.

I got kissed by a pig-shooter out on my walk. John Lockley, who shoots here, one-time head wrangler for the *Lord of the Rings*, expert horse-rider, pig-dog breeder, brought some Opotiki pig-shooters for a day out. I met them on the laneway, and this great big man in a Swanndri leapt out from the back seat and gave me a big kiss to say thank you. Who says chivalry is dead?

Pig-shooters are driving me mad. The phone rings every other day. Yesterday I had a call from someone called Pig Dog. Last week it was two young guys with dreads and nose rings. I think I'll give them a day. Kit had dreads and a nose ring.

Dear Virginia

I hate everything to do with pig hunting. I hate the fact small dogs tear at the legs of huge pigs, like pulling on guy ropes. I hate the way pigs scream during their bloody death fight. I hate the way men carry pigs over their backs and the blood covers them.

In contrast, on the regular Sunday walk with Jane we met steers and a large kune kune pig out the back of Makara. To meet a few steers on a narrow track, with a fence on one side and either another fence or a gully on the other — what do you do? We have been known to just turn around and walk back. But this time we had to go on, as we were about two hours away from the car and it was 3pm and we'd be getting back in the dark if we didn't get past these huge creatures. They walked ahead of us down the track, fences on both sides. Each time we got close to them they swung around and glared as us, and we froze. At last we got to a place where there was what I'd call a layby. We walked close to the opposite fence. I tried to shout in a farmerly way. Little squeaks came out. The cattle lumbered into the passing lane, which they probably regarded as a lunch stop, being as there was grass there rather than scrub and tussock. We walked past as quickly as we could without looking as though we were hurrying. Ridiculous, really, but what do you do?

Hello, Janice

You have to show animals that you are in charge or they'll take liberties, like those steers ambling along in front of your Sunday stroll. Steers are silly animals; they're like teenage boys but without the testosterone. If you had charged at them shouting and waving your walking pole in an authoritative sort of a way, they would have skedaddled in panic. I love the way steers crowd around you in a paddock, they get closer and closer, jostling each other for a better look, pouting and snorting; if you were a city person you would think you were about to die, but if you know steers you crouch down very still and wait until they creep very, very close — and then you leap into the air like a bumblebee on a spring and shout 'Bizzzzz' and they all fall over each other in the rush to get away.

Dear Virginia

On the drive home from dinner last night I heard the last lines of the Garrison Keillor show. He said: 'Never wave your arms and shout at large animals.'

Hello, Janice

If you believe that Lake Woebegone man you'll believe anything. Of course you can wave your arms at big animals, but you have to do it the right way — there are wrong ways and you learn from experience.

The rain is unbelievable. I do not remember when we last had such rain, maybe ten years ago. I wonder how many plants will get bogged and die. I don't remember when I last wished for a clothes drier, but it was probably when I was still washing nappies in the wringer washing machine. I have rigged up a drying room in the washhouse to dry a two-week backlog.

We were scanning the ewes today; it was vile. The rain just pissed down, mid-morning it tried to snow, the mud rose in the yards like a thick brown custard, the sheep were water-logged. The beardy dogs were water-logged. Poor Toby couldn't jump the yards, so heavy was his coat, and the ground a soup with no consistency for take-off and he's old. Just a vile day.

I imagine it is raining in Thorndon and that you are curled up by the heater today.

Dear Virginia

Yes, curled up with the computer and still racked with 'Shall I/Shan't I' indecision. I've upped my licorice supply. I received an email today inviting me to the delights of the Tokyo Book Fair . . . *Expose yourself to over 40,000 visitors and 500 exhibitors to generate lucrative business.*

Last night I looked through recipe books to find inexpensive dinner menus. I'm imagining life without the security of a salary. Will I have to eat lentils all the time? I did come across something interesting. Did you know that in English — which you and I use but bureaucrats don't use any more — the names of domestic animals are Saxon and their cooked flesh is Norman? Ox, steer, cow, calf, deer, swine, fowl, sheep — as opposed to beef, veal, venison, pork, pullet, mutton. This shows that after the Norman Conquest the Saxons worked raising the animals that the Normans then ate.

Hello, Janice

The temperature at Double Tops has now risen to 6 degrees, so I am thinking of putting on some wet-weather gear and taking the mountain bike out for a spin. July is a devious, cruel month. Another four days and it will be over. Only then will I feel safe from snow, frost, rain and sleet. The sun is growing stronger and the oystercatchers have returned, a sign that spring is coming. Imagine if it didn't. I suppose that is why our ancestors sacrificed virgins and stuff, just to ensure that it did.

The hunting season is over, too. Harry has survived another year. I imagine horrible leg or neck breakages when Harry is away hunting, especially since I learned that his nickname is Helicopter Harry. He assures me he never takes risks, but I know he is exhilarated by speed so I don't believe him. The hunting season concludes with a dinner-dance to which we do not go. Once upon a time the hunt used to host a ball. I went to one once, in 1968, an occasion I will never forget. I had never seen so many posh drunks gathered under one roof, and I was accused of being a brazen hussy by a woman who thought I was trying to seduce her husband. The man was a fiendish groper from whose grasping embrace I was attempting to extricate myself. I think that is why I've never been brave enough to return to an end-of-year function at the Brackenfield.

August

Dear Virginia

(Written in a warm café.) Everyone seems to have gone overseas on holiday! Robert told me yesterday he had a swim in a lake in the North West Territories somewhere — in 30 degree (C) temperature. 30 degrees! The Arctic summer is hotter than our own summer. Somehow I didn't think that should be so. But the water, apparently, was very, very cold.

Dear Janice

Tell Robert swimming in Yellowknife would be good for the health. I have Danish friends who swim for their health between the ice floes. They have to wrap up as soon as they get out of the water or their togs freeze onto their skins.

Sunshine died last week — of milk fever. She developed it while we were away skiing, and by the time we returned she was in the star-gazing phase. I gave her a subcutaneous injection of calcium borogluconate and a dose of Ketol. She rallied a little but wouldn't eat. She died two days later. She was the most affectionate of my sheep and the only one who enjoyed being caressed. She would press her face close to mine in a gesture of friendship, which was sweet. The rest of the flock care only for food. We cannot dig graves for all our pet animals, so poor old Sunshine was dropped down the gut hole. I feel so sad.

Dear Virginia

I will try to cheer you up by telling you about work trips overseas. A trip overseas is a perk few people get to sample, but those who do like to tell us what colour green the grass is over there. What greater honour could there be than to be a representative of your company, at a conference in Florida, Tunisia, Zimbabwe, the Solomons, Frankfurt, Beijing? The overseas trip is the sign that you have been accepted into the power nucleus of the company. When I hung my head over the divider between two cubicles yesterday, and interrupted Steve teaching Emma how to use chopsticks by demonstrating with two pencils and a rubber, I knew she had been selected for her first marketing trip to Japan.

'You'll have a great time,' I said.

In Zimbabwe, Don found paper made from elephant dung. He thought it'd be perfect for writing those difficult letters to various clients: to Ministries, to the city council, to the Tax Dept. The pad of paper came complete with a crude graphic of an elephant on a toilet seat. When he brought it through Customs it was confiscated. A few days later it arrived, neatly repackaged by Customs, all cleared. Don is offering to sell individual sheets of it, with his editorial services thrown in free.

Don is the employee most renowned for his overseas eating exploits. It's bad enough going to a conference in Auckland and having to watch him eat a cooked breakfast with all the tomatoes, mushrooms, bacon, hash browns, eggs and sausages you can fit on a plate. It is much more seriously anorexia-inducing if you travel with him overseas. In Zimbabwe, Don ate everything on the menu. He reports that crocodile tasted like a fishy chicken with a salmon bone down the middle. Ostrich was like beef. Dried eland in peanut sauce was not nice. Goat stew was also not nice. Zebra was the worst — tough and slimy. He passed on warthog.

Not only is Don known for relishing telling us his food stories, he enjoys telling them when people are tucking into a team morning tea. This results in no one eating much of anything, even the chocolate cake specially made by Margaret. Word soon gets out to other staff that there's cake left on the trolley in the kitchen. The raptors, led by Rupert, descend. Rupert can dive at thrilling speed from a great height to clamp the last piece of anything in his long, beautifully manicured fingers.

Don's visit to Niue coincided with the fruit bat and wood pigeon season. For breakfast people simply shot six pigeons. Six was considered a serving. With fruit bats you eat the whole thing, even the wings, even the singed fur and the head, turned on its side with little clenched teeth. After you've bitten off the head and the fur, the thing that's left exudes a greenish black oil with a very strong taste.

Here is Don's recipe.

Shoot fruit bats.
Gut and singe fur.
Wrap in banana leaf.
Cook in umu several hours.
Dig up and eat.

Conferences in the US pose a different problem for Kiwis. There is no drinkable coffee. There is never anything being sold on the food stalls in conference venues that resembles food as we know it. The only stall that sold anything half-real at one conference was selling baked potatoes (all symmetrical). The Kiwis subsisted on this one stall until they could go to the NZ trade mission drinks — where they were noticeable because their fists and cheeks were full of carrot sticks and fruit kebabs.

A little interchange I thought you'd like: on a plane returning home from the States, a colleague sat next to a leather exporter who told her old cows are better for leather than young ones. 'Old ones have the most interesting patterns.'

'Why?'

'Producing calves. It stretches them.'

Hello, Janice

I was thinking about bureaucrats going off-shore in the winter as I tried to rouse the energy to ring yet another couple to ask how their cruise went. I have endured so many mouth-watering descriptions of tropical beaches, yachts, snorkelling among rainbows of fish, the Yangtze River, the Greek islands, Tuscany, that my salivary glands have quite dried up. It's very unfriendly towards the planet to zoom all over it every six months in a jet plane, but then all these people probably feel very enviro-friendly because they use eco lightbulbs and take cloth bags to the supermarket. So bearing this in mind, my friend Oonah and I went travelling with the International Film Festival yesterday.

We began travelling that way thirty years ago; ie, we have been going to film festivals together for thirty years. Oonah is now almost eighty, but still has the stamina to see three movies in one day and go out for dinner afterwards *and* walk the stairs to the eighth floor of the car park. Travelling via the movies doesn't burn tons of fossil fuel and you get to meet the natives up real close. Yesterday we visited Norway, Canada and Paris.

Tomorrow the shearers arrive to crutch the paddock sheep. I thawed two chickens for lunch — and then the weather forecast told me that snow will begin falling at nine tomorrow, and what do I do with two chickens that will not be needed because the shed-full of dry sheep will not last until lunchtime? Turn the chickens into a stew and put them back in the freezer. What a bugger.

Dear Virginia

In Wellington we warm our souls in bitter weather by seeking out the conviviality of a cozy café. When someone takes you somewhere new, shows you a hidden little round table for two, orders you a drink you've never had before — that's almost an expedition, and you become the explorer. Today Dan took me to Schoc, a café I hadn't been to before. It's on Tory Street and I've always walked right past it because I like Meat, a bit further down. Meat is unique as it's a café in a butcher's shop. They have the best sausage rolls.

Dan introduced me to Schoc's Chili Choc, a Mayan hot-chocolate drink that must be wonderful for commuters from the train or the ferry who need that prickly heat inside them before facing the lifts that take them to their offices. There's a lump of pure chilli chocolate in the bottom of the cup. You suck the drink, with this slowly dissolving chocolate, through a long-handled spoon that acts as a straw. The drink was rich. Fat makes me drowsy. I staggered off, warm inside, to snooze through yet another meeting.

My pet hate is cafés that keep their doors open. And I don't like cafés that serve huge muffins instead of small scones. I love the Momo bowls in Eat, I love the tiny Afghans in Smith's the Grocer's. I love the rhubarb pastries in Nikau.

Last week we ordered in a café and took our plastic number tile to the table to insert it in the wire holder. I noticed it was number eighty-nine; or was it sixty-eight, I wondered? The workmate I was with is pregnant. She told me the new rules: no raw egg, thus no mayo or aioli, no Hollandaise, no salad unless made by herself, no soft cheese. All hard cheeses and all dairy, including butter and yoghurt, have to be no more than two days old after opening. I was astonished. She needed iron, she said. I offered silverbeet from the garden. She said she'd keep taking her supplements. Then the waiter delivered my coffee and her herb tea, and turned our number upside down before lifting it up and taking it away.

Hello, Janice

This afternoon there was a knock on the door and there stood a man with one leg with an elbow crutch supporting the stump. He was the underneath-the-woolshed cleaner man. It took him thirteen hours @ $100 an hour plus GST to clean a few years' accumulation of dung from beneath the slats. He lies on his side and operates a giant vacuum cleaner that sucks it into a tank thing. He told me it's a great job. He doesn't have to stand, or sit at a desk, and he says he must be one of the few men in New Zealand to be paid for being in the shit every day. After I had written the cheque he asked me if he could come deer stalking one weekend, and I said certainly but did he put his leg on to stalk deer — to which he replied that he didn't because his stump was too short to wear a leg. 'But,' he said, 'I take two crutches. It makes things a bit easier.'

Years ago we did employ a one-armed painter *and* paper-hanger to paint the house. He rode up to Double Tops every Monday morning on his motorbike. He lived with us for the week, and my biggest nightmare was trying to get the dishes dried before he could offer to help, because he used to tuck the wet dish under his stump pit and dry it with a tea towel in his working hand. Some years after he worked for us he rode up to see us, and on the way home he tipped off his bike as he turned onto the main road. The people first on the scene panicked when they saw he only had one arm and began looking for a severed arm on the side of the road, until a woman who was a nurse happened on the scene. She looked at the one-armed man but saw no blood. 'How many arms did you start out with this morning?' she asked, and he mumbled, 'Only one.'

Dear Virginia

My increased purchasing of licorice, peanuts, and chocolate consumables has swamped the top shelf of my pull-out pantry.

That umbilical cord which links me to work, and through which my lifeblood flows, has become stretched to breaking point. I am what we call 'stressed'.

I asked my manager how I go about purchasing an essential piece of equipment. She sighed, tired, as always, and named someone who had bought new assets recently and maybe I should ask him. 'He might know what form to fill in. And you'll have to make a business case to Finance. All I know is that you have to use bullet points. Finance likes them. And you need lots of signatures.'

I am sure no cattle, grumpy cow or spoilt pet sheep could be as difficult as an asset-controller in a large company. I fantasize about mustering them onto a cold south-facing slope and leaving them there all winter. It's time to resign, if only I were brave enough; resign and go on a diet, or stay and grow bitter and massively overweight.

Hello, Janice

Purchasing assets at Double Tops is done differently. I went out to the deep-freeze two weeks ago and noticed the bread was soft, then I noticed the deep-freeze wheezing like a patient in the terminal stages of a lung disease. 'I need a new deep-freeze,' I said to Harry. The overdraft is humungously huge, but he just said, 'Go and buy one.' I rang around the shops in Christchurch, negotiated a cash price, and a transport price, paid for it on-line.

Days went by. I rang again. They had forgotten. Next day the transport rang to say a deep-freeze was arriving that afternoon.

It arrived on a huge truck driven by the skinniest man you have ever seen: I was wondering how he and I were going to unload this huge deep-freeze, when Harry arrived and together he and the skinny man lifted it off. Then Smiths City rang to say that my deep-freeze would be arriving next day. 'One has already arrived,' I said. 'Oh, do you want two?' the lady asked. At $1,800 each I didn't think so.

PS: The one-legged deer-stalker is coming stalking this weekend.

Dear Virginia

I have noticed that several times you refer to your deep-freeze — a thing I call a 'freezer'. You visit it in times of distress, when emergency rations are required, when unexpected guests arrive, or when harvests are bounteous. Let me tell you what is in my freezer.

First, you have to imagine it. It isn't a huge white box, gently humming in some back room, surrounded by gumboots and Agee preserving jars. It is merely part of my fridge. Because my kitchen is small enough for me to reach everything in it without having to walk more than two steps, there is no room for a large fridge, much less a separate freezer. So meet my fridge, the narrowest model on the market, covered in plastic fridge-magnet words from Shakespeare.

At eye-level is the freezer section, with its own separate door. Inside is one shelf, dividing the space into two layers. The first holds about fifteen plastic pottles — they used to be yoghurt containers but now they contain the cat's food. I never, ever, run out of cat food. Whenever steak is relatively cheap in the supermarket I do a swoop and buy it up. I lug it home, not over my shoulder as your hunters do, but in my supermarket bags. I then spend an hour chopping the meat into bite-sized chunks and filling the pottles. The cat watches this procedure; he is glad I have a freezer.

On the shelf above is a big plastic bag. Woe betide any visitor who rifles through the bag looking for some quick and delicious snack. What they will find looks more like evidence of a murder. Inside are grisly remains of rejected cat meals, or our leftovers that are too smelly or greasy to be composted. Every week this bag is dumped in the rubbish bin just before it is collected.

Occasionally there might be some ice cream in the freezer as well. That's all. I tend to use the supermarket as both my kitchen cupboards and my freezer.

Hello, Janice

I have never called the deep-freeze a freezer. I suppose it's pedantic but I don't like 'freezer'. I don't like the word veggie either, I like vegetable. My deep-freeze sits out in the garage. It is too large to keep in the kitchen. I don't know how many cubic litres it is, but it is big enough to store a corpse in if you folded the legs before rigor mortis set in. It holds a very large steer, chopped into bits, with ease. If Harry ever goes missing now, you'll think, 'I wonder if he's been chopped into little bits and frozen?'

Anyway, my deep-freeze usually contains neat packages of steak and great rolls of roast beef and corned beef for shearing, and mutton legs and shoulders and wild pork legs and venison steaks. As well as all this meat, the deep-freeze holds emergency supplies of milk and bread, vegetables, berries, pastry of all kinds, root ginger, lemon grass, chillies, unsalted butter, chicken stock, fish, and of course ice cream. Chest deep-freezes are awkward because, no matter how well you think you have stacked them, the item you want is always at the bottom.

The deep-freeze also holds a treasured gadget I forgot to mention: an ice cream churn. Fresh ice creams, *granitas* and sorbets are a very special treat. I have a small deep-freeze at the bottom of the kitchen fridge that is probably the size of your freezer. In it I keep the things I use the most. My deep-freeze is to me what the weekend supermarket is to you: a source of emergency supplies when unexpected visitors call.

Dear Virginia

To take my mind off the image of Harry folded up in the deep freeze, I will tell you about cakes. Office workers love cakes. Cakes and computers go together. You can get ridiculously expensive cupcakes that look more like something you'd wear on your head rather than put in your mouth. Would you like me to bring you one when I visit? Do they have them in Christchurch? They are all the rage in Wellington now. This is because an office worker needs frequent injections of caffeine. Coffee is an appetite suppressant. You don't want a bowl of bone soup or slow-roasted mutton with your coffee, but a little cake — that's just the ticket. So coffee and cake is the staple food of the office worker.

I love delicious, sweet things that work well with coffee, instead of having a bread-heavy lunch — lime *crème brulée* with rhubarb *compôte*, chocolate cake with raspberry *coulis*, frangipani pie, or Neenish tarts.

Cafés don't do sandwiches any more. They seem to deal only in hinged bread — *ficelle*, *fergosa*, *panini*, *ciabatta*, etc. Sliced Vogels just doesn't do it.

Overheard on Featherstone Street on my way to a café meeting: two brawny guys with orange vests on, who'd been moving road barriers, walking past: 'No, it's not Thai pasta. It's different. It's noodles. You have to soak them, not boil them.'

And off they went.

Hello, Janice

I have no idea what a *fergosa* is, or a *ficelle*. The *panini* reached Hawarden some time ago but obviously we still await the *fergosa*.

Have you gone to a tropical island? It is a while since I've heard from you. If you have, I do not want to hear anything at all about it. At Double Tops the snow is slowly melting from the hills, but I see the temperature has fallen to −3 tonight and it is only 9pm; the snow will lie on the shady faces for a few days yet.

Poor Fleur is training for an adventure race in China. She leaves in two weeks' time; it is very difficult for her to train to race in very warm temperatures, so yesterday, to simulate the

Sichuan province in late summer, we stoked the living-room fire to white-hot heat and put the electric heater on high. We raised the room temperature to 33 degrees, then Fleur got on her bicycle wind-trainer and cycled for two hours. I was lying on the hearth mat watching television, and I almost passed out whilst Fleur cycled on, with sweat dripping from her body onto towels spread on the floor.

This weekend was the Waikari School's pig-hunting competition weekend; the road was crawling with pig-shooters. The Romano boys stayed in the shearers' quarters and roamed all over Double Tops in the snow and mud, but caught only one pig, an 80-lb boar, probably not big enough to make an impression. Whilst they were scouring the eastern side of the farm for the elusive prize-winning boar this morning, we were mustering West Mjolfjel. Harry said his dogs, Meg and Cap, discovered a mob of pigs and bolted after them instead of chasing sheep.

My dogs and I did not disturb any pigs, but we did walk over huge boar-rootings in the valley floor. If I were a serious pig-tracker I would have got down on hands and knees and smelt the spore — The Terryfier does that, and when he does he spends quite a time with his nose to the ground and then he says 'Yesterday' or 'This morning.' Terry has a very good nose. So good that when he is on exercises with the Territorials he is placed in the advance party because he can smell the enemy at 100 paces.

The pig-shooters often ask me if I would like a pig for the deep-freeze. Mostly I decline, because accepting a pig means that I will have to skin it, which takes a very long time. A pig does not skin easily as a sheep does — you have to kind of cut the skin off. The other reason I decline is because mostly the pigs are too big. If someone offers you a pig, do not accept it unless it is a small one. I know it is unlikely that you will be offered a pig, but on the other hand I remember that pigs were seen in the Wellington green-belt which kind of goes past the back of your little street.

In case a pig-shooter does kill a pig in your back garden, I think I should tell you how to cook it. Large boars and old sows taste disgusting, and as they are scavengers you just do not know what they have been eating. I always remember our neighbour Bill telling me that his wife would say, 'Mmm this pork is so delicious', and all he could think of was the putrid cow the pigs had been feasting on; this is a slight deterrent to eating wild pork.

So, if a shooter offers you a wild pig and the pig is a large one, chop it up and throw it in the rubbish tin. If the pig is small, cut it up and put it in the fridge. The best joint on a small pig is the saddle. A saddle is not a fashionable cut these days, so you will most likely never have seen one. I guess that is because it uses all the loin chops on both sides of the spine. To get your saddle, do not saw the carcass in half until you have removed the whole lower back. The saddle is the lower back, and it is the most tender and juicy cut on the carcass. Wild pork is a dry meat because there is usually very little fat in it. To roast the saddle, I put it in a covered meat dish with 2–3 tbsp olive oil, a handful of sage and another of thyme, a whole root of garlic, and enough small onions for each diner. I serve the pork with garlic-mashed potato (take the garlic out of the roasting dish and squash it into the cooked potato), sweet peppered carrots, green vegetables and, of course, stewed apples.

Dear Virginia

I feel sorry for the wild pigs of North Canterbury. We do not hunt pigs in the CBD. But there is a hunting, of sorts. It takes place at lunchtimes and, like fox-hunting, requires a large group of hunters and never enough things to be hunted.

It's a high-adrenaline adventure, hunting down a lunch in the jostling, buzzy streets in the CBD. We know they'll be empty by 2.30, when you could skateboard happily down Lambton Quay without interfering with any traffic. But at lunchtime, you could imagine you are in New York. If you sit on a stool at the Fuel Bar in the BNZ building, where skylights let you look up the high glass sides of another skyscraper next door, you really do feel you are somewhere bigger, more urban. The food court, under the BNZ, is like any food court, in any shopping mall, anywhere. Lunchtime is high tide, with a wave of hungry office workers curving down the escalator, hunting for sushi, Mexican, Indian, pizza, rolls, cakes, Chinese, kebabs, and kai.

If you are running from the madness of the over-decorated, over-priced cupcakes, you can still find the ordinary bakeries operating out of shoe-box-sized premises down side streets. You can find them easily at lunchtime, because there's always a queue of office workers shuffling slowly into the shop and then coming out with a brown paper bag. Favourite things in these shops are egg sandwiches — just plain egg sandwiches — or ham sandwiches, and of course pies, rolls, Afghans and custard squares.

Hello, Janice

Do not feel the tiniest bit sorry for wild pigs. They are vicious animals, they like eating little lambs; did you know that old sows and boars develop a taste for new-born lambs? Pigs are smart; elderly pigs know that fresh, delicious, warm lambs drop out the back end of a ewe — they develop a nose for a ewe about to give birth and they stalk her, after the lamb is born they snort on in and gobble it up. Remember poor Olivia, the pet lamb who was so cleanly eaten by Emma the pet pig? Well, an old sow can chomp her way through several Olivias a night.

Snow is falling on the lawn — again. I have lost count of how many snow falls there have been this winter, of how many times the Double Tops block has been a great white hummock, of how many postponements of the crutching we have had; but at least we are not trying to shear. That would be a great deal worse. Yesterday as I sat buffeted by a chilly wind on the top of the Milo block, every farm to the west of us was white; it was as if I stood on the verge of the Southern Alps. The hills, usually brown and calm, looked savage and cold, like mountains with rugged black ridges showing between the snow-drenched ravines; the sky was pale blue, streaked by a ragged nor'west arch. I was mesmerized by the wretched cruel beauty of winter — and then I drifted off, I'm a great dreamer.

Mustering involves waiting: because musterers work in unison, you do not get too far ahead of each other or the sheep might slip between the cordon. As the junior musterer I usually wait much longer than Harry does; I used to get frustrated and sit grumpily looking at my watch, but now I sit and look at the shifting sky and hawks and skylarks and falcons and I dream, sometimes I return to the past. Yesterday I was back in the Double Tops winter kitchen almost thirty years ago with a table full of shearers sitting around a huge mutton roast. I remembered all the days when they did not shear because of the rain and snowstorms; days when they drove down to the pub for the day and returned for dinner full of booze and bravado and scheming about how they were going to 'do the electrics'. Our gang was a blade-shearing gang, and they were referred to as the 'scissors' by the local shearers who were all electric. There was much rivalry and ribaldry between the gangs on wet days down at the tavern.

Ginny at the end of the road is coping with snow-disrupted shearing and two small children, just like I was all those years ago, and my reveries on the Milo tops led me to bake a batch of hogget pies for her deep-freeze. Pies for the deep-freeze are a substitute for takeaways on those days when you are too tired to cook. Takeaways are not an option out here in the hills.

Hogget Pies

Take a leg of fresh hogget and dice it. Coat the meat with a handful of flour and brown in 2 tbsp of oil. When the meat is browned, pour a glass of red wine into the pan, and then add 1 large chopped red onion, 4 cloves of crushed garlic, 6 chopped carrots, salt to taste, and 1 tsp of white pepper. Add a cup of water and simmer the stew until the meat is tender — around about 1½ hours. Then add 2 cups of chopped button mushrooms and simmer a little longer. If the stew is too sloppy for a pie filling, reduce the liquid a little by turning up the heat — but stir it!

That is the pie filling. Hogget stews are great as you can stew whatever you happen to have in the fridge, pantry or garden; hence the mushrooms, red onions and carrots. I know the conventional method is to lightly brown the onions and the garlic first, and then brown the meat, but in this self-devised recipe I have eliminated this step as browning onions and garlic is always dodgy if you are in a hurry. I suppose the stew/pie filling is a kind of hogget version of *coq au vin* or *beef bourguignon* (but without bacon) — both use red wine, onions, garlic and mushrooms. It is always handy to have a bottle of red wine to pour into meat stews or casseroles; the wine I used was a Pinot called 'The Miner's Wife'. It was not an expensive bottle of wine.

To make the pies, roll out 2 packets of flaky pastry. Line the pie dishes, fill with hogget stew, top with a pastry lid, egg-wash the pastry, and follow the baking instructions on the pastry packet. This recipe made 6 small pies and 1 large one. Think of the planet when you use pastry and do not buy the pre-rolled; each sheet of pastry is accompanied by a sheet of plastic, which you throw away.

PS: We have just received an email from Fleur. She is in Wulong, in the Sichuan province of China. Today at lunch she decided not to try the green chillies fried in chilli oil, or the hen's feet. Tomorrow she begins a four-day adventure race in a team with three Swedish guys. Time to try the more bizarre dishes after the race is over.

Dear Virginia

I could probably run as fast as Fleur if I fuelled up on chillies fried in chilli oil.

Talking about running fast, I was thinking today about how

we in the city work hard at deceiving ourselves that we are soooo busy all the time. We all rush rush rush to work in the morning, grabbing a coffee en route. The rubbish bins on The Terrace and Lambton Quay are full of cardboard coffee cups by 9am. Rush rush rush home after 5pm, via the supermarket. 'Hi, so and so. How's it going? Busy? I know. I'm just soooo flat out', grab the pasta and the milk and the wine, rush rush rush home. BUT — during the working day there is always time for a long leisurely café coffee, maybe even two. It's called a meeting.

Here are some of the meetings of the last few days. All involved eating and talking at the same time. None of them involved hen's feet or chillies fried in chilli oil.

Had lunch at Higher Taste, the Hare Krishna place in the old BNZ building with Fraser Williamson, an illustrator who does idiosyncratic figures in profile, surfboards, fish and palm trees. He's just come back from Morocco, Spain, France — all the boring places, and he's throwing all his stuff into a big box and going off to his wife's Tongan family in Nukualofa for six months. We talked about Morocco and Spain and mosques and tile patterns and arches and domes and Tonga, and publishers.

I had a drink with Annie, director of NZ Drama School, at Astoria at 4.30. She told me about a party she'd been to, with a pre-revolutionary French theme.

'You couldn't hire a powdered wig in town for love or money that night,' she said.

I felt dull.

Yesterday I lunched at Word of Mouth where I met Cathy who works for Caritas, the Catholic social welfare agency. She said one of her co-workers had resigned. Sigh. 'Hard to replace her. We need someone with Spanish and Swahili.'

The day before that I had a kebab — the best in the

Wellington area — at Aladdin's in Mana, near where the Mana-to-Picton ferry used to leave from in the days when Robert was the captain. I was with David, from the studio. We were in a queue behind a blonde young thing. She turned and left, clutching her kebab in the white paper wrapper, and David and the Turkish guy groaned and gloated at each other with shared appreciation. Then the Turkish guy remembered I was also a customer and asked, 'And what would you like, princess?' He really pushed the 'princess'.

'A large beef, and lots of onion,' I said. I usually get a small beef and no onion.

A few days before I'd been at Pravda, drinking Sauvignon with Maxine, who came to the café bundled up with a large pillow. 'Going to a concert, the Fauré, at St Mary's,' she said. It made complete sense. Everyone pads themselves up for St Mary's rock-hard seats.

On Saturday I went to lunch with Ray. He said that when he's working — in a Roger Hall at Circa at the moment — he always eats his main dinner at lunchtime. So I did, too. Then I went home and fell asleep on the couch. This is the life of a Wellingtonian whose job depends on the quality of her networks.

Hello, Janice

You won't be able to eat out every day when you are self-employed — unless you become a consultant.

Yesterday was race day at Mt Lyford. It was a beautiful day. I wish I'd treasured it more.

A day of days! I let it come and go
As traceless as a thaw of bygone snow
It seemed to mean so little, meant so much;

Christina Rossetti, from 'I Wish I Could Remember
That First Day'

Remember the owl I wrote about, the little owl I thought
was a harbinger of doom? All winter it mocked me from
the pines at dusk. Every night when I walked through
the trees to feed my dogs in their kennels it cried its
mournful, derisory cry and I hated it all the more.
That bloody owl was mocking me, my world has just
fallen apart. On Sunday night Harry came in to the kitchen
and said, 'Look at my legs.' His beautiful slender ankles had
been engulfed in flesh, they looked like elephant legs. I knew
straight away what was wrong. Kidneys. Now we have begun
the hospital thing, blood tests, ultrasound, X-rays, a biopsy. So,
you see, Saturday, which I thought a nice but unremarkable
day, was the last day of being able to take Harry's health for
granted.

I know I shouldn't be worried. It is a useless sort of emotion,
but I'm still worried. The only way to counter doom and gloom
is to see the funny side, and the funny side is that Harry has to
go on a very low sodium — salt — and potassium diet. A low-
salt diet means eliminating everything that tastes good. Low
potassium eliminates nearly everything else. You should see the
list of forbidden foods. All cheeses except cottage, all sauces
and pickles, salami, olives, tomatoes, bananas, even Marmite
and peanut butter.

Low salt means boring, insipid, tedious, dreary, deadly and
dull. I'm always restrained with salt, but now I shall have to be

zealously frugal, so my letters will be full of imaginative ways of making dishes taste good without any salt. How lucky that I have a herb garden, and how lucky that we eat salad most nights; I can make mayonnaise or French dressing without salt.

I am bloody mad at that owl and the world that is so relentless in conjuring bad surprises just as we are on the cusp of success. I want to go out and scream and cry and smash things, but it is a beautiful sunny day so I shall go into the garden and 'make my hands busy to keep the world at bay'.

September

Hello, Janice

Thanks for your two letters. Writing is great therapy for me, I spent half the week going back to the bloody owl letter, writing what I really felt then taking it all out again; like hitting a punch bag. We spent Friday night in the ED at Christchurch Hospital. What a parade of sad humanity. Harry is out on leave, and I take him back to hospital tonight for more IV drugs and tests tomorrow.

Adding to the gloom, we received a letter from PGG which was sent to all their farming clients; they say that the fundamental issue for us all is that sheep farming in New Zealand is no longer profitable and that the current season is likely to be one of the worst in real terms in fifty years. Farmers are leaving the industry in large numbers, putting the industry's very sustainability in doubt, and this is in spite of a global boom in agriculture — it goes on. It is a very gloomy letter.

And now Fleur has emailed from China to say she has broken her finger. She broke it sometime during her race, in the cave section she thinks. She says it is very swollen and sore; she raced for the last two days with it in a splint! Fleur's story had a funny ending. The official sports doctor told her that she needed to see an expert who would be there after tea. When she returned to meet the expert, she was greeted by the *same* doctor. He was now wearing a white coat. Appearance is everything.

Off out farming now, onwards and upwards. Please write to me of salty things, I want to know that they still exist.

Dear Virginia

I'm really sorry things are at a low ebb. When we can't cope, here in the city, we can always take a sickie. But when you live your work you can't do this, and any small disability, like aching muscles, tiredness, etc, affects all aspects of your life. I can understand how such a sudden, and major, illness changes everything. I hope the hospital can do something helpful and that Harry feels better soon.

As requested, I will write about salty things. How about takeaways? I rarely have them because I know it takes less time to make an omelette and salad, or steak, or pasta, than it does to go down to the local fish-and-chip shop where you have to queue outside in all weathers and wait for your order to be cooked while avoiding eye contact with everyone else in the queue. But I do have them occasionally when I'm at a studio and we've run into the dinner hour and we need a break. Phil's studio is partial to a fish-and-chip break, or an Indian. David's studio always and only goes for kebabs.

This weekend I came back from Bill's with brother-in-law, Hugh, and his youngest son, Judge, who introduced me to Subway sandwiches at Waiouru.

'Honey Wheat bread, please.'

'None left.' I chose another bread.

'Cheese, please.'

'None left.'

'Oh. Ham?'

'We only have chicken left.'

'Oh.'

I didn't dare ask for a coffee. I couldn't risk disappointment. I couldn't be responsible for what I might do.

We laughed about this, parked up outside the Waiouru Army Museum. On display in that museum is the canteen truck that school children raised money to buy for the Maori Battalion in World War Two. I'm sure Te Rau Aroha — that's its name — never ran out of food. It has dents and bullet holes in it, caused by enemy fire, not by irate customers demanding service.

Get well, Harry!

Hello, Janice

Last week I thought of Bunsen. I was driving past the Masons Flat garage, slowed for the intersection then looked into the garage, as one does, to see who was there. 'At' (Alistair) Lawrence's Toyota was parked on an angle, and sitting up in the passenger seat at a slovenly angle sat Buzz, At's elderly and portly Labrador. He was fast asleep with his mouth ajar.

Dear Virginia

This letter is to amuse Harry. It's instead of my visiting his bedside with grapes. This is virtual food, and it's about food.

When I wrote about studio lunches it got me thinking about lunches in the office.

What an office worker spends on her lunch bears no relation to her salary. Often the CEO can be seen in the staff room nibbling home-made sandwiches quickly like a guinea pig, while the receptionist or the IT guy might go to a café or a pub and spend $25.

The simplest lunch is still the sandwich. David C usually brings a peanut-butter sandwich. He says: 'It's really quick to make, which seems like a good idea when I'm making it and running late, and then turns into a bad idea when I pull it out of my briefcase and it's slightly squashed and slightly dry and everyone else in the staff room is making up very fancy salads using exotic ingredients.'

Some people always bring leftovers. They never hang out in cafés with cupcakes or *ficelles*. They bring in stew or fried rice or lasagna or mince or chop suey, stir-fry, bacon and egg pie, or macaroni cheese, each dollop in its own plastic pottle. They put it in the fridge then heat it up for lunch.

(I have never done this, but I do have a fine collection of plastic pottles at home — re-used Greek yoghurt containers are the best — for storing my cat's rejected breakfast in, so I can offer it to him again in the evening, this time with a candle and napkin . . . When Stephan was staying with me last year, he used to take my precious pottles to work — he was a leftovers man — and never bring them back! The cat and I got very upset about this.)

The office fridge receives all these varied and somehow very intimate little plastic pottles every morning, and woe betide anyone who mistakenly microwaves the wrong one at lunch-time. Some people label their pottles; some don't. In every workplace there are unsolved cold cases of serial pottle theft.

Sometimes someone will leave their lunch in the fridge and then they will have to work through lunch, or they will be invited out on an unexpected date for lunch, and they forget their humble pottle in the fridge. It will stay there for days, weeks, until it explodes with a massive fungal mould frothing out from its plastic-sealed lips. Many all-staff emails have variants of *Urgent: Fridge Clean Up Needed* in their subject line. They are some of the most passionate emails sent around the company. It could be a cajoling email: *Puh'lease don't leave food in the fridge after it's started to get a life.* Or the situation will become critical: *Last Chance: fridge is being cleaned out of mouldy or expired 'food' in 5 minutes.* War is declared when it gets personal: *No. MY mince had corn AND peas in it! So there!*

Other high-octane emails concern smells in the fridge. The packed-lunch banana is often a culprit here. The staff room can so easily become a place full of over-wrought people arguing over a brown banana or an unclaimed pottle of pesto. That's when office humour is needed. Last week, in the middle of a hygiene dispute, I opened the fridge and a pat of butter fell out at my feet. Immediately an accounts person said, 'Looks like assault and buttery to me.' Crisis averted. By humour.

At lunchtime the 'leftovers' people make a coffee while their shadow of last night's dinner is heating up in one of the microwaves, then they might sit at a circular staff-room table and read the paper and eat. Today David had *dhal* and rice, but he didn't have on hand the cashews, raisins, yoghurt, tomatoes, chutneys and poppadoms they had with it last night, so it was a major disappointment. Such are the sad moments in an office worker's day.

After microwaving, some eat their food out of the now-very-soft pottle. Others transfer the contents to a bowl or plate. It's amazing how often you notice someone trying to pile far too much food onto a far too small plate. Yet others take their steaming pottles back to their desks and get back into the sunny fresh air of Googleland and Facebookland for the rest of their all-too-brief lunch hour. Unless their reheated meal was sardine pasta, that is. Anything *redolent of food*, says the notice on the staff-room noticeboard, *MUST be eaten in the staff room and not where other people are working, where it may offend.*

The one small bench in the staff room is taken over by the assemblers. They are the discerning eaters. They don't like much-cooked food, and they hate it all melded together, as in a gravy or sauce or stew. They don't like soggy or gloppy. They come with knives and little graters and lots of pottles and plastic bags. In the bags are salads, bean sprouts, maybe cheese, maybe tofu. In another large plastic sealable bag they might have bread. Hinged bread or Turkish flat breads are popular. They find the only clean large plate left in the staff room, lay out the bread, make an artwork in the centre of it with cheese, or maybe a tiny can of chicken or tuna. They carefully scatter bean sprouts over this, or sunflower seeds, then they cover the mound with hummus from a shop-bought pottle. Dressing, from a tiny bottle, is dripped over it. All the containers are carefully pressed back together. Then the bread is wrapped up into a roll and a hunt is on for the one and only sharp knife. Meredith brings her own. She also, along with about a quarter of all the workers, has her own plunger and her own coffee, too. All assemblers are female.

The staff room really becomes a fully functioning short-order canteen when Paora and Stormy arrive, with steaks and eggs and big bread rolls. Pregnant Kelly, who is only into raisin toast for lunch at the moment, skitters out of the staff room and leaves the guys to it. The staff room doesn't have windows that open or a range hood or extractor fan. P and S cook up their steaks on the toasted-sandwich maker. Then they fry the eggs on it too. The haze and the evaporated fat stays around for the afternoon.

This all sounds a long way away from making hogget pies, mustering, or waiting in A and E all night or nursing Harry. I am thinking of you both.

Hello, Janice

I never knew that lunch was such a complex matter in the office and that it occasioned so much conflict. I didn't realize how much time office people devote to planning what to eat for lunch. How do you account for this in those fifteen-minute timesheets? I didn't know that bitter refrigerator wars could erupt from lunch storage, either.

All your lunches sound salty and yummy and very, very dangerous. We have been made to be aware and afraid of the evils of salt since Harry's frightening fluid retention; poor Harry was so full of fluid he looked like a jelly baby. He is beginning to shrink — slightly. He has something called Minimal Change Disease, a kidney disorder, which in most cases is resolved with a course of prednisone and other drugs. This means a continuation of low-salt eating until further notice.

Lunch at Double Tops is a simple meal, open sandwiches. I acquired the open-sandwich habit in Norway, where we ate rye bread, brown goat cheese, salami and pickles — every day — for breakfast and lunch. At Double Tops we make our sandwiches with cheese and salami and lots of salad vegetables. I guess Harry will have to cut out the salami and hard cheese and make do with vegetables and cottage cheese. Low-salt eating is like being thrown into a dungeon and left to survive on bread and water. It is a diet of deprivation. The advisory sheet from the dietician says to avoid foods with more than 450mg of sodium per 100g. So, take yourself off to your pantry and read some labels — you will be very shocked.

Commercial bread contains 450mg of salt per 100g, but as I make all the bread we eat I can make a low-salt version and that will allow me to use a little more salt elsewhere.

Bloody owl, as soon as I heard that sinister bird hooting I knew it presaged some sort of crisis. They said my great-grandmother had the 'second sight', which might explain why I hear portents in the cries of owls. Harry thinks I'm quite mad. This may well be true.

Dear Virginia

I do hope Harry recovers quickly. It sounds a nightmare. I wish there was something I could do.

Something to make you see owls differently, not as harbingers of doom, but rather as hapless animals grossly manipulated by politically correct humans without brains: I received yesterday lyrics for a song someone was hoping I'd record. The composer wrote: *I am enclosing a song about a hungry morepork who, despite his hunger, has respect for the sustainability of the creatures he eats.*

Today I think my mind is working the way it does when I see those horrific pictures on the anti-smoking ads and immediately want a cigarette. Something in my brain said

Salt is Bad, and I went shopping for a salt grinder! The shop was overheated by a huge heat-pump. What does it feel like to work in that discomfort, standing up all day long, dealing with dithering people like me who might not even want a salt grinder? I maybe wanted an avocado slicer. I ended up with both, because it was so hot and the assistant had swollen ankles and feet, which I don't think was caused by kidney disease. My credit card was 'unrecognized' by the EFTPOS machine. 'Because it's hot,' the girl said. She put Sellotape over the strip on the card.

'Hey, mind my card,' I said. 'It's kind of precious to me.'

'My sister keeps hers in the freezer,' she said.

My potatoes are up and I've draped them with the new compost from the bins. Some peas are up, but a friend tells me I should have planted them in April. She has pods on hers! But the best thing is a little teepee surrounding some peas. It's made of three straight, thin sticks from the plum tree's pruning in June. Astonishingly, these sticks have blossom sprouting from them, all down them, like buttons.

If you can think an owl is a portent, then I can think the sprouting plum prunings are portents, too — new, healthy beginnings for Harry. With the peas growing underneath, my little teepee is very cute — and remarkable. I'm sure every perfect potager will want a blossoming pea frame. I also have a row of beetroot, carrots, chives and lettuce. My silverbeet is huge. Spring must be a time for the beginning of new, good things.

Hello, Janice

It is five weeks since Harry showed me his elephant legs. His ankles are thin again and he is getting better, slowly. I do not feel as burdened with responsibility for the farm as I did when he could barely crawl out of bed, but I *am* burdened by the low-salt regime. I can cope with no salt in the vegetables and I haven't put a salt cellar on the table for years — but a *tagine* without salt, a stir-fry without fish sauce, *risotto* without chicken stock? They are all pallid, insipid versions of their true selves. And then there are the salt zealots, worse than reformed smokers. 'Oh, but we haven't cooked with salt for years,' they smirk; they are intolerable and oh so morally superior, but I bet they eat bacon and salami and olives and Parmesan cheese.

I'm not going to dwell on what I cannot enjoy, I'm going to tell you about a love affair.

A love affair can sneak up on you unawares and tap you gently on the shoulder, or it can thump into your heart like an electric fence thunderbolt on a wet morning. I still remember the thump to my heart when I fell in love.

It happened on a dull winter's afternoon in a dingy room at Templeton Hospital and Training School. After I trained as an Occupational Therapist, I was appointed to Templeton as a sole-charge therapist. I had never worked with intellectually handicapped children and I didn't understand how a big institution worked, either. I took over a staff of three OT aides, and a general factotum named Peter Young. Peter was the most loyal assistant anyone could ever have, he looked after my interests and I grew very fond of him. He had been a resident since he was a very small boy, and he knew how to work the system — extremely well: it took me a good while to catch up with him.

The hospital was a closed community, with male villas to the east of the administration hub and female villas to the west. A barter system operated between the patients and between the villas, and until I learned it the OT department was the recipient of many gifts from the villa kitchens. I slowly discovered that Peter was selling my favours all around the hospital in exchange for scones and cakes and dried apricots and other goodies. 'Miss Sinclair sends you a hug and a kiss' was his standard line. Peter's barter system extended to the travelling salesmen who supplied the canteen. We were showered with ice creams, sweets and chocolate bars, and that is how I met Bernie the Cadbury man. He came to see the girl who was sending him hugs and kisses in exchange for chocolate bars.

Bernie and I got talking over a cup of tea and gingernuts. Gingernuts were standard Mental Health Department fare along with the tobacco issue. Yes, tobacco — tobacco was issued once a week in tight, white-paper packets bearing a Department of Mental Health stamp. Tobacco was a tradable commodity for those who did not smoke, the gingernuts were not. They are an odious biscuit. Anyway, I told Bernie I was covering crystallized ginger and candied orange peel with chocolate. He asked what sort of chocolate I was using, and when I told him I was buying cakes of Energy chocolate he said he could get me a 5lb block of dark couverture which would be a superior chocolate and save a lot of money. The day he delivered the block of dark chocolate to the OT department was the day I fell deeply in love — with chocolate, not with Bernie; Bernie was a very married man.

I'll tell you how to make chocolates some day when my mind is fresh. I have a very good truffle recipe which you can use to make after-dinner delights.

A frost this morning and the roses showing signs of

pain. Lambing begins this week; I cannot believe it will soon be ear-clipping time again. Office work with Neenish tarts sounds attractive.

Dear Virginia

I was asked to lunch by Frano, the wife of Michael, a man I used to work with a long time ago. She's English, a great cook, and a keen gardener. She creates beautiful spaces and places. She has an artist's eye, and just makes things happen. She has liver cancer, and her sister had come from England to see her. They reminisced about Christopher Lloyd, the great English gardener, whom they stayed with when they were young. Christopher once got Frano to make a salad, from the garden, with nasturtium and borage flowers on top. She made the salad as instructed and dressed it with the specially prepared vinaigrette. Christo picked all the hundreds of little bits of borage and nasturtium flowers off the dressed salad before it got to the table, because he said that a salad with flowers must never be dressed all together. You make the salad, dress it, then scatter the flowers on top. That way they don't go limp with the oil. Breakfasts at Great Dixter always featured a huge crystal bowl full of stewed garden fruit. When Frano visited once in the fig season, he said, 'Let's be fig pigs', and they went off to eat figs from the tree.

In Frano's dining room we lingered over the pickled cherries, which I first mistook for olives. They are an Elizabeth David recipe. But I'm sure they are not on Harry's diet list for the immediate future. It was a wonderful afternoon with spirited people who know how to live, no matter how much time they might have in which to practise this art.

Hello, Janice

My father died of liver cancer. He didn't tell anyone about it until two weeks before he died, I think he'd rather lost his enthusiasm for life after my mother died and didn't want treatment. He rang one evening and said, 'Virginia, I'm going to die', and I said, 'Oh, would you like me to come and say goodbye?' and he said, 'Yes that would be nice.' And that was it. He died ten days later and only the last two days were nasty.

I do know salad flowers should be sprinkled on after the dressing — the oil turns them limp and transparent. In the middle of the winter, rocket flowers are a nutty addition to salad. Farm cooks use what they have to hand, which is how very odd salad recipes develop. I made a salad with beetroot leaves and rocket, finely sliced red onion, orange segments, toasted walnuts and rocket flowers.

I nurtured the tiniest lamb I've ever seen yesterday and today, before it went to heaven. I'm sure if its mother could speak she would have asked for the words *A Little Angel Only Lent* to be inscribed on its tombstone. He was the most perfect fluffy white lamb with pink nose and ears and beseeching soft grey eyes; he weighed 900g. Harry found him, along with his twin, on Sunday night. He decided the other twin might make it and confined him with his mother in the cow bale, he left the comatose angel for dead wrapped in hay on the back of the truck. In the morning the angel had arisen, so Harry brought him in to the kitchen. We were shearing and I had a hell of a busy morning cooking for ten with not a thing prepared, but I managed to rush out and catch my hogget who I had relieved of a dead lamb the day before. Poor hogget; I milked a small bottle of colostrum from her tight, sore udder. I drip-fed the angel, then wrapped him in a towel and laid him in front of the heater. He spent a wonderful day sitting in front of the heater like a cat. Henry the dachshund had to spend the day outside as he insisted on subjecting the lamb to gross sexual harassment. This morning the angel was a little off-colour and he died just after lunch. His twin died also. They were slightly premature, just not robust enough for this world.

I have a pet calf. We found her abandoned at the south-west track junction on the way to Voss, a little like finding a lost child at a railway station, so of course we have named her Pumpkin, after the little girl abandoned in the Melbourne railway station. I've also picked up two lambs whose mothers died of *Salmonella* after drinking pond water in which an old ewe decided to commit suicide. The lambs are Marrow and Zucchini. As well as Pumpkin, Marrow and Zucchini, I'm subsidizing seven lambs in the front paddock. It's been a tough year and many sheep with twins cannot make enough milk for two lambs. If you teach the lambs in the first few days of life that you are an extra mother, they accept you as a source of milk and will come running when you sing the feeding song. It does look very funny when I 'bleat' and all these lambs rush to me leaving their anxious mothers bleating for them to come back, just like the good mothers of Hamlin town.

The broad beans are flowering, and I do have lettuces and mesclun mix growing and broccoli waiting to be planted out, but the plants have to be covered with netting to keep the hares off. We have run out of ammunition and cannot buy any more until Harry renews his gun licence, which he keeps postponing because last time he got a gun licence they said it was for life. If it was for life, why should I have to renew it? he asks. I tell him 'rules is rules' and that you cannot fight bureaucracy, and that if we want more ammo he'll have to succumb. I'm envious of your garden and must get my potatoes in or they won't be ready for Christmas. I'm sure there is not a huge advantage in early peas.

Must go. Got to go to work. The farm is holding together. The bloody diet is killing me with boredom. Protein is not wise either, so there is little left to look forward to, and I'm doing the diet too as it seems a bit cruel to eat what Harry cannot. The prednisone is making Harry very excitable.

Janice is due to calve any day now. I will inform you the minute the offspring arrives.

Dear Virginia

I thought I'd take my time, put in some effort, and produce a carefully wrought sonnet for you this week. It's my equivalent to your cheese-making. It's about the Café Colleens who escape for a quick sip, away from computer screens and To Do Lists and Meeting Maker. I hope it's an antidote to the prednisone.

The Café Colleens are the big spenders of the office. They dine out. They are the $15 lunch set. The Café Colleens discuss, via many emails, where they will go that day. When they get there, there's lots of queuing, lots of deciding. Which hinged bread shall we have today? A little *ficelle* or a *ciabatta* or a *croissant*? Dried tomatoes and feta? Roast pumpkin and rosemary? Chorizo and rocket? And, of course, a coffee. Trim soy latte or trim flat white? A few minutes to eat, then lots of gossiping — which is encouraged somehow when you're in a noisy room with lots of other Café Colleens all doing exactly the same thing.

Me? Which group am I in? Am I a reheater, an assembler, or a Café Colleen? I'm one of the Café Colleens. I always go out. I spend a ridiculous percentage of my earnings on eating out. The breads always disappoint me, but I love the desserts. And I love the chatter and the clatter of it all. And these days I prefer to be out of the office. I could never eat my lunch in the staff room.

Office Desk Sonnet

What next? Ohmygawd! Check the iCal. A coffee window!
Leave the project clutter, and the admin infill,
Gather the pod mates, email the IT god, and text
The bosomy bureaucrats from the old team at the Min.
Go! Go to the chatter and chirp and clatter of the café.
'I was dying.' 'Enlarge my world.' 'What's the goss? . . .'
    'Puh-lease!'
'I could go a Beehive cupcake.' 'Or a James Cook club
    sandwich?' 'Eh?
Black pants wiggle on shiny seats. No bosses. Ahhh. At ease.

*

Outside, craggy hill hands cradle the big latte bowl of the
    harbour.
Glass buildings sparkle like cocktails, cranes poking out their
    tops
And waving, waving. Then, 'See yer see yer,' quardle the
    coffee queens

Crossing Lambton Quay under the sky's big blue screen
Thinking little thoughts about office chores, office bores
Shrinking to fit behind their own small PC screens once
  more.

Hello, Janice

I'm pleased to announce that after a short labour Janice gave birth to a fine black calf at 5pm this afternoon. This morning I thought she would calve some time during the day, because rather than join Doris and Boris at breakfast she took herself off to a high knob in the paddock. I drove past at three-thirty this afternoon and saw that she was turning in small circles and looking every now and then at the grass as if she were expecting the calf to have dropped out. I stopped the Niva, wound down the window and yelled at her to 'push'. She just stared back at me as if I didn't know what I was talking about. Harry was passing about five and he observed the intimate moment of the birth through his binoculars.

I visited her as the light was fading. She is a very proud mother, and the calf is clean and well licked — all over. I didn't get close, as it is unwise to approach a cow straight after the birth. They are unpredictable, even friendly cows like Janice. As for the horrid Doris, the first time she calved she disliked her calf so much she bellowed and stamped and screamed and tossed it in the air. We were surprised the calf survived the ordeal.

I have no energy to write more, and certainly no energy to even contemplate writing a sonnet; I'm impressed that you have written one. I seem to have been trudging through mud and shifting breaks and hoggets and ewes and lambs for days and days on end.

I am looking forward to your Christchurch visit on Suffrage Day. I've never spoken in front of a group of people before. I'm a bit nervous. We'll have to have a glass of wine beforehand.

Dear Virginia

Two glasses.

Text from J

At Art Gallery. Great building! Good coffee too. Where do we meet?

Text from V

Driving past in 5. Drinks at Arts Centre and prepare what we're going to say. Nervous.

Text from J

Don't be.

Text from V

How many people will be there?

Text from J

No idea. Thousands!

Hello, Janice

We enjoyed your visit, and hope you were not exhausted by the flow of farming information. Several friends I talked to on Monday were concerned that you saw a flower show that was a pale shadow of a city flower show. Little Jonah, the calf, is doing well. It's a good name you gave him.

Dear Virginia

I loved visiting Double Tops. And it was great to see Harry looking less like a jelly baby and more like a farmer. Tell the Hawarden Tourism and Publicity Department, Flower Show Sub-committee, that they needn't worry about my reaction to the flower show. I saw it differently. Everyone who came up to you asked 'How's Harry?' before they said anything else. It sounds a bit overblown, but I did feel that your community accepts life's vicissitudes and helps each other. My only concern about the visit was that I didn't do anything useful at all, except opening a few gates. I loved the dinner with Dugald and Mandy, especially the miniature meringues.

I will remember it all, especially getting up in the morning and waltzing into the kitchen and seeing you there, teapot at the ready — and the Titan oven on, lit from the inside, and there, through the glass, I saw rows of perfectly formed tiny cone-shaped meringues. That is being busy!

October

Dear Virginia

I have a shopping list three pages long. Tomorrow I go shopping for the party ingredients for the combined Robert-Hugh-Janice birthday party. Robert came back to New Zealand especially for the event. His next job is in Fiji. It's now rare for all the family to be together.

We are having many delicious spreads to put on 'crusty' bread — recipe-book-talk here — to keep people alive until they have all arrived, so feta and fennel, white bean and garlic, pea and mint, beetroot *hummus* (which I discovered from the Julie Le Clerc book you sent me), olives, etc. I fear for my carpet. But the combination, on a large platter, of a mound of pink beetroot *hummus*, another of feta and fennel (which is white), and another of pea and mint (green) is wonderful to look at. Then we'll have either salmon kebabs (on one BBQ) or steak kebabs (on another). The vegetarians amongst us have specified that they can't eat vegetarian fare cooked on the same BBQ as the meat. Robert and all his cousins — none of whom would ever be vegetarian — will be kept busy working out how to use the new BBQ and being chefs. I will tell them one thing: don't keep turning the meat over and moving it around. Leave it to cook!

The tiny kitchen will be freed up for the salads and sauces. The oven will have hot bread in it — I am thinking of how I will grate 5 cups of cheese for the cheese and garlic spread to put on the loaves. The recipe says the bread is 'great for teenagers', so its purpose is to keep the ravenous nephews happily munching on the deck. I think I will reduce the amount of dairy product, for the good of the nephews' health and my bank balance. There will be a giant platter of asparagus, too, because of the season.

The dining room will have the food laid out in it. But people won't be able to eat there as it is far too small. The laundry will be transformed into a bar — complete with fairy lights. The laundry was made into a large 'wet' room when Bunsen was ageing. It was the place for drying muddy dogs. Now it makes a perfect bar. Get your drink and walk straight out into the garden. After a recent plumbing disaster, the floor in the laundry and bathroom is what guys call 'dodgy', so I hope no one falls through.

The carnivores will gather around the BBQs. I have one huge pot of freesias which is the best feature of the garden at the moment, so other people, including vegetarians, can gather around that. There will be tables with extra food in other rooms, to prevent starvation as people set off on expeditions around the house. All the doors into the garden will be open. It will be fine weather . . . impossible to predict. The forecast shows both rain, and cloud without rain. Hmmm.

The dessert will be a giant chocolate cake in the shape of an electric guitar, coloured red. I have ordered this from Dorothy's Cake Shop — one of Wellington's institutions. It has been in the same place in Cuba Street ever since my first trip to Wellington, as a school girl from Gisborne on a Careers Guidance course. The last cake I ordered from there was a replica of a wheel — for Robert's twenty-first.

I hope there will be enough food and that it all works out. I hope I don't have too much food, and heaps of leftovers. You just never know. Right now it is pouring with rain. The freesias will be battered to bits. Robert has lost his cellphone and is uncontactable. Someone has just phoned to say they are vegan. And — worst thing — there is absolutely nowhere to park in the whole of Thorndon.

I've spent two days doing writing workshops for ten- to thirteen-year-olds in the Katherine Mansfield House — a frigid, gloomy Victorian pile. We took over the whole house and the kids explored the weird artifacts like taxidermied birds in glass jars, huge 'baths' hanging on the kitchen wall, irons so heavy the kids could hardly lift them off the stove, the same with the jelly moulds. The beds upstairs are so narrow you can't imagine adults sleeping in them. The bedrooms also contain chamber pots, sewing kits and hat boxes. In the kitchen the kids loved the bottle of laxative, and I pored over the handwritten recipe books. The recipes looked exactly like the ones in my mother's recipe books. Same ingredients, same handwriting. Do you remember writing recipes down in a notebook when you were a young wife? I do. Now I have a shelf of favorite recipe books and a huge pile of recipes torn from magazines that I'll never organize into a properly accessible file.

Must go. Need to sleep before the day of the party.

Good evening, Janice

The wind has finally stilled in the hills back of Hawarden, but as the weather system is slowly clearing from the south I imagine the winds in Wellington will still be strong enough to extinguish the barbeque flames. I hope no one falls through the laundry floor and that the nephews do not starve before the meat is cooked, and that the carpet is not soiled with squashed beetroot hummus. I'm sure the party will be a raging success.

I am in need of victim support. Is there victim support for traumatized gardeners? There has to be; I need counselling. Yesterday I was admiring a newly flowering rhododendron bush; it was a mass of stunning, dark-red trumpets. This morning the jealous wind sucked up a whole section of the trellis fence and hurled it on to the rhododendron and killed it dead by snapping it off at ground level. It savaged the five rugosa roses which I had just planted out. The rugosas are not dead, but they are severely mutilated. I am a victim of the wind; I hope he will be kinder to your party than he was to my rhododendrons, otherwise you will need more than counselling. I advise getting seriously drunk.

Dear Virginia

Hmm. Counselling is difficult. In letters it always sounds vacuous. I need to stride in and pour you a whisky.

I will try to find cheerful ways to raise your blood-alcohol levels and hence your spirits. We were at the Flying Burrito Brothers the evening before the party — and had to wait for a table. I sat at the bar and watched blackly dressed women picking their way around puddles in their high heels as they crossed the road to dine in Logan Brown. I decided these women are the CBD's equivalent of estuarine stilts; I also decided on a G and T. Haven't had one in years. And it was bliss, so much better than Chardonnay.

Then two nights later, after I'd been in A and E for four

hours — yes, I, too, am in need of victim support — a sister-in-law, Rowan, introduced me to a combination of the following three things: Lindauer, free-flow frozen berries, and a vacuum cap for a champagne bottle. In her household they always have a capped bottle of Lindauer ready and waiting for a quick after-work pick-me-up. So that's my counselling for those moments when the trellis is flung onto the rhodo by the wind: bubbly drinks, with free-flow frozen berries added.

Now, for more counselling, two stories about the wind. Today the wind was so strong it would have been impossible to walk across the motorway bridge. As I had a presentation to make at a government department, Susan, the project manager, came to my house and we hired a cab to drive us across the motorway bridge and another one-and-a-half windswept blocks to the Ministry. We arrived ten minutes early because the taxi was faster than walking. That was fine: they invited us to share their pod's morning coffee session (home-made ginger kisses), with the quick quiz from the *Dom Post*. Between the eight of us we were able to answer all but one of the questions. It was: which country invented Neenish tarts? The answer is Australia, and none of us knew.

The other wind story is the most recent story of Don and his travels. The Pacific workshop in Suva wound up with an (Irish) farewell blessing given by a Marshalese Islander in which he slightly changed the words 'May the wind be at your back' to 'May the wind be at your backside'. Don took this as just a mistake in the art of translating; but later, when he had food poisoning, he was advised by a Fijian healer there to use Vicks VapoRub, a whole jar, as a suppository. It was then that the blessing took on a more sinister meaning.

The party. I was going to tell you about the party. The wind magically died down. The fairy lights sparkled in the pergola.

Robert was fully occupied with the BBQ and the kebabs — which were very good indeed. I know they weren't made with such high-quality meat as the ones I had at Double Tops, but I compensated for that with a marinade of cumin and coriander and soy, and I made a jug of peanut sauce which all the nephews loved. The most popular salad was a carrot and coconut and currants salad. The secret to this was that the currants were soaked overnight in wine vinegar and honey. The huge platter of asparagus that Peta brought just disappeared. And all those Julie Le Clerc dips were great — especially the feta and fennel. While the adults were trying exotic salads, the young ones were eating the hot bread. Tricia brought an amazing *tiramasu* (no idea how to spell), and the full-size electric-guitar cake came complete with tuning pegs.

It's been a week for birthday parties. Ralph, a life-long drama teacher, was seventy. At his party, in a massive penthouse apartment with glass walls, an opera singer, in a flame-coloured ball gown, sang his favourite arias. Laughton and Jenny sang Cole Porter standards with very unstandard lyrics. Vincent Ward Skyped in from Bangkok, and someone told a story about Ralph looking after a lost young English student some years back. The young student was Orlando Bloom. And this weekend I go to National Park where Bill has his big party at Marie's Restaurant. I need there to be a month of no birthdays soon, in order for me to rest up.

The morning after our party Robert cleaned up all the empties, the recycling, the leftovers, and did all the dishes. He took me to A and E where I was X-rayed because I'd fallen over and smashed my shoulder. It is not broken, just 'separated'. Then he went to his new job in Fiji.

The next day, feeling very delicate, I looked at the garden most of the day. The sun shone. There was no wind. I noticed the potatoes are thriving. The carrot and beetroot seedlings are showing. The broad beans have vanished. The garden is blue, from inky ajuga and columbines, to soft honeyworts, and then to bright forget-me-nots. I love the ajuga — so deep, so regimental-looking, such a contrast to the tumble of the honeywort. And there are splashes of Dublin Bay red, lots of pink stocks, and, best of all, under the snowball tree's white pompoms are ten blue irises. A perfect birthday present.

Hello, Janice

A glass penthouse and an opera singer, how glamorous. No one in the least bit famous has Skyped into our living room lately. Gay dropped by yesterday for a cup of tea; she used to live up the steep end of the Virginia Road and now she lives in the city. She's not quite as famous as Vincent Ward, but I mention her because she sucked the wind into her lungs and said, 'Oh, how I miss the country air.' Gay has turned into a city person; city people dream of life in the country with fresh clean air, but I know they wouldn't survive on clean air for long. Your letters are always of parties in penthouses, work colleagues and meetings, coffee and cafés, Friday drinks and weekend dinners, delis and bakeries. You would shrivel and die here, like a lettuce plant without water — so would Gay.

Fresh air is quiet and The Rocking Frog with its espresso machine is a long way away. Most visitors are bird-brained and usually in feathers (but not Gay). A pair of kereru visits each morning to dine on laburnum shoots, a pukeko is contemplating a garden inspection — an alarming prospect — and yesterday

I met a pair of paradise ducks waddling up the drive. As for entertaining, the thought of hosting a dinner or a lunch party without salt fills me with such despair I cannot begin to think about it.

I've stuck my nose in a book instead. The book is *Belgian Chocolates* and the author is a man named Roger Geerts. The book is hardly for everyday use, unless you are a professional *chocolatier* or, like me, a chocolate nutter. Last month I think I said I'd tell you about learning to temper chocolate. Tempering is the process you put chocolate through to make it snappy and shiny, and it was something I always wanted to learn first-hand.

It's funny how life works out. I finally learned how to temper chocolate on an institutional stainless-steel bench in the kitchen of a school boarding house. This was years after Bernie and the chocolate block, and it came about because I was invited to help the Director of Boarding at Fleur's school select a new catering manager. After receiving a deluge of applications, Angela and I drew up a shortlist of four. An ex-army chef, two hospital-trained dieticians, and a long shot, a German hotel chef. We interviewed the German chef first, and were immediately smitten with his beautiful smile and very impressed with his credentials: he had cooked in famous hotels, he could do vegetarian, he had studied nutrition, and his menus were imaginative. But why did he want to work in a girls' boarding school? we asked. He told us he wanted a day job so he could be home with his children whilst his dessert-chef wife worked nights.

After interviewing the army chef and the very suitable and very sensible hospital-trained dieticians, we selected the German chef. Our selection was subject to review by a registered dietician, who of course recommended either of the sensible hospital-trained dieticians. Angela and I had the final say, and after reviewing the dietician's recommendation we appointed the German chef with the lovely smile and the gourmet experience. Daniel was a great success as catering manager, and the school served the best food in town. Kate, the dessert-chef wife, was also a *chocolatière*; she was my tempering tutor in the boarding-house kitchen and we have been friends ever since. Kate and Daniel now own their own restaurant, Megawatt, in Christchurch, and they help me with hard-to-find ingredients for chocolate-making. It is enormously helpful to know someone in the restaurant trade who has access to ingredients that never appear on the shelves of a supermarket or, if they do, sell at hugely inflated prices.

Chocolate tempering is messy. It took me ages to learn the art of efficient tempering, and when I first began I managed to smear the whole kitchen and myself with chocolate. I think that unless you have the chocolate passion, it is tidier to go out and buy the chocolates. But here is a recipe for truffles; they are easy to make and a great after-dinner standby for any drop-in celebs.

Chocolate Liqueur Truffles

500g chocolate
200ml cream
50g unsalted butter
2 tbsp liquid glucose
2 tbsp liqueur

The secret weapon is the liquid glucose: it makes the truffles melt in your mouth, do not leave it out. Liquid glucose is now available in the baking section at the supermarket.

In a heavy-bottomed saucepan, heat the cream and butter.

When they are almost boiling, take the pot off the heat and add the glucose and chocolate — broken into small pieces — stir until the chocolate has completely melted. When the mixture is cool, add the liqueur and beat the mixture with a wooden spoon — just a little bit or it will become too fluffy.

Line a shallow square sponge tin with baking paper and pour the truffle mixture into it. Leave to set for 24 hours.

When the mixture is firm, cut it into squares, roll the squares into balls. At this stage you can roll the balls in good cocoa powder and leave them to dry on baking paper, or you can be tricky and dip them in melted chocolate. Melt your chocolate in a bowl over a water bath (never let the water boil), then wait until the chocolate is lukewarm and dip your truffles.

I did not specify the chocolate or the liqueur as it depends what sort of truffle you like. You can use all dark, all milk, half of each, half-milk, half-white, all white — just play around each time you make truffles. The better-quality chocolate you use, the better the finished truffle will be. My favourite liqueurs are Baileys, Kahlua and Cointreau — not all together, of course. If you wish to add more liqueur to make the truffles taste stronger, you have to drop the cream content and up the butter slightly, otherwise the truffles won't set.

Dear Virginia

Effort! My god! It isn't how much time we have left, but rather how we choose to spend the time we have in the here and now.

Some of us make quilts, some of us restore railway carriages, strip down engines, play guitar — and some of us make cheese and chocolate, or meringues before breakfast, ready for a seemingly effortless dinner. The truffles you sent were divine, even though they took ten days to get here! We have feasted on them and I will try making them, when I have hunted down the liquid glucose.

The weekend after the party, Rowan and Wayne went off in their camper van to Scott's Ferry, whitebaiting. Hugh and a son went up to Horopito to continue restoring the railway carriages they have on land up there. Robert settled in at Nadi. And, unable to drive because of the shoulder, I went to Bill's — on the train.

I was at the station at 6.30am. No time for coffee or breakfast. Each one of us travellers was told, individually, as though we were in a doctor's consultation room, that there was no train from Wellington that day. There had been a derailment. We were going to Palmerston North on a bus. And so we did. No coffee or food on the bus. Not allowed. I was hoping there'd be some refreshments at Palmy. There hadn't been anything open in Wellington's railway station.

In Palmerston we waited for the engine to be shunted onto the train. We waited some more. Then we got on. After about ten minutes the train manager came on the intercom and announced that the buffet car, in car B, would be open for service just as soon as he'd unpacked it.

'As I was the person putting all your luggage in the luggage van, I haven't had a chance to attend to the buffet car yet. I will let you know when . . .' He suggested we might like to look at the menu in the pocket in front of us. I did. The menu said the sammis were conceived by Logan Brown. I just knew that it wouldn't be the same as dining in their great restaurant in Cuba

Street. I decided to save myself for Bill's lunch.

Ten minutes later he's back again, announcing that the buffet car is open for business.

'Unfortunately, due to the espresso machine breaking down, we are unable to serve coffee on this service today.'

Oh. No. I slump into a caffeine-deprivation coma in my seat.

At Ohakune we are an hour late, but we are nearly at National Park. I'll only be an hour late for Bill's special lunch. I sit up. The station manager's cheerful crackle comes back.

'We will stop here for lunch. The train will continue its journey in one hour.'

So there I was, half an hour away from National Park, except it was one-and-a-half hours. I had a speech to make at Bill's birthday. I was sharing this task with Tessa; she was waiting for me at National Park station. When the train pulled in to National Park at 2pm, I was desperate for coffee, desperate for lunch — I hadn't eaten in Ohakune because of the anticipated delights of Marie's catering. Tessa somehow managed to get lost in National Park and we went round and round the block looking for Marie's. We both know the big restaurant very well. It made no sense.

When I staggered in to the birthday do, the lunch had been cleared away and they were laying pyramids of cupcakes on the tables and organizing the arrival of the birthday cake. No breakfast and no lunch for me that day. Bill handed me a large glass of wine and the speeches began. I think I delivered one. I don't remember.

I finally ate at 8pm when we all sat down to a magnificent impromptu dinner at Bill's — beef fillet and salads — put together by the amazing and unflappable caterer, Marie, at National Park.

Hello, Janice

No series of food letters would be complete without a story about the main trunk line. 'Taumaranui, Taumaranui on the main trunk line.' I did think things had got better since the old days of the Limited and the Express, but maybe not.

We have just finished a day's tailing in the wind. At and Sue were tailing too, right on our boundary, so we drove over to yahoo at them. They are a generation younger than we are, but there has always been much friendly ribaldry between us, usually over the merits of the horse versus the motorbike, or the virtues of our Lada Nivas which make At apoplectic. Last time I saw Sue she was dressed to kill at a party; today she was dressed to tail. What a leveller tailing is: dirty clothes, blood spatters on your face, shitty hands, wind-burnt skin, hat hair, clumpy boots, thick socks . . . There is no way you can look glamorous — unless you are Jane Clark-Hall. You didn't meet Jane, but she is a neighbouring farmer who can make even the grubbiest tailing-overall look glamorous. It's very annoying and I do not know what the secret is.

Dear Virginia

Office clothes are probably not as varied as tailing clothes. For men they are totally uniform — a grey suit. And for women it's usually black trousers with everything, and often a black jacket. Very drab. Rupert does try to brighten our office up a little. I saw him today standing under the air-con vent by the stairwell.

'To get my hair boofy,' he said.

We are all meant to keep a spare set of clothes — for emergencies — in our earthquake kits. One fashion-conscious young editor replenishes hers regularly, when she's changing the water bottles and batteries, so her earthquake clothes won't be out of fashion by the time the Big One strikes.

Dear Janice

Good news! Harry has been given permission to resume a normal salt intake, so maybe there will be joy in cooking again and maybe a lunch party to write about. Harry is better in the meantime. The odious owl has flown. My beautiful kereru sits in the laburnums with his mate, and the shining cuckoos have returned from the Solomon Islands and the Bismarck Archipelago where they spend the winter. Spring is truly here. I might have a dinner party, a candle-lit and salty dinner party, with lots of wine and good conversation.

I learned about dinner parties and conversation as a teenager in Wellington. My favourite cook and hostess was Mother's friend Cormie O'Shea, who lived in Ngaio. In her house, coffee and conversation seemed to be available at any time of the day and night. We stayed with the O'Sheas whenever we visited Wellington, and I loved it. To a Gisborne girl it was close to Bohemia. There was always a big gathering around the dining table where guests would sit arguing long into the morning.

Cormie's husband, John, made films, and the guests around the table were invariably volatile, articulate and exciting. As an incubating adult, I would sit amidst the smoky air, twirling my wineglass, silently smoking whilst formulating brilliant replies to questions that never came, like a redundant tennis player to whom the ball was never served. I loved those dinner parties and imagined that when I grew up I would host such dinner parties . . .

Dear Virginia

I am so glad Harry is better; 'better' being defined as 'being able to eat salt'. I hope you have your dinner party and that the table is surrounded by deipnosophists.

It's warm — yes, actually warm, and still. The tuis and blackbirds are singing and it is time for dinner. To celebrate Harry's return to health, I'm sending you some office ways of preparing for disasters, medical or otherwise.

We recently held a competition to see who had the best earthquake kit. Michael won with a kit that included safety ropes, camp cooker and emergency blanket. Sylvia was awarded the 'good neighbour' prize because she was the only person who had deodorant in her kit. Anne won the 'Lifestyle Award' for bringing tins of smoked salmon. Phillipa won the 'Mission Impossible Award' for having tins of food and no tin-opener. Simon won the 'Impractical and Perishable Award' for his cheese and crackers. One team ordered twelve cartons containing 144 bottles of water. Now they don't know where to store them. Water is heavy. When people leave work it is considered good form to bequeath your kit to the new person, rather than taking all those baked beans and canned peaches home.

An office worker spends a lot of time being trained for all sorts of unlikely eventualities: difficult clients, resolution of conflicts, career planning, presentations in foreign places, and emergencies of a more cataclysmic sort. They don't learn how to control a charging cow, or how to temper chocolate. We have just endured a Civil Defence Day. We staged a re-enactment of a bad-day-at-the-office scenario.

Tricia spent the day slumped in a lift thinking she had a tibia protruding from her left leg and a jagged piece of metal in her right. Dianne was folded up in a corner by the photocopier nursing a collapsed lung and a yard of intestines. Sarah lay on the concrete floor in the basement for hours bleeding from stomach wounds and developing hypothermia. Tricia and Emma were hauled up and down stairs, tied precariously to stretchers with loose bowlines and half-hitches. Emma remembers, hazily, someone shouting 'We're losing her!' as knots gave way and she nearly plummeted headlong down the stairs. Tricia soothed her shattered nerves by watching the *Titanic* movie in the evening.

Sylvia and David returned to work the next day, a resurrection miracle as they had both been pronounced dead the day before. In the essential post-mortem meeting, David said, 'I learnt that, when in doubt, amputate.' Everyone has been warned to give him a wide berth if they have a headache.

Thank god Harry is on the mend. I don't think you'd like one of our newly trained medical emergency team helping out.

November

Hello, Janice

Once a year Kate and Vicki, proprietors of The Rocking Frog, organize a charity auction; I mentioned The Rocking Frog back in March as being our nearest coffee shop. It is a classy little coffee house where locals and passers-by can drop in for a good coffee or a glass of wine and something to eat. It is also an art gallery. Last year, local men were asked to create an artwork for the auction. I think you would be surprised at the originality of some of the works. There were one or two genuinely good pieces made by real craftsmen. The rest were — um — surprising. Harry made a work out of a dried cowpat spray-painted with gold, with five black and orange jellybeans stuck in the centre. This was mounted on a black board with white McCahon-type writing which said something very profound about the meaning of life. Someone bought it for their loo.

Jim Greenslade, the auctioneer for Peter Walsh & Associates, conducted the auction. He was very dangerous. You didn't dare scratch your nose or catch his eye or you might find yourself assigned a hundred-dollar bid on an item of very strange artistic merit. The most expensive item of the night was a Waikari farmer, Sam, plus his digger. Sam's wife, Di, offered him as her artwork. He stood before the assembled crowd looking bashful whilst Jim extolled his many virtues — in bull-sale terminology. Four hours of Sam plus his big digger were knocked down for $480.

This year it was the women's turn. On Friday morning I

began making a rose and strawberry ice bowl for serving ice cream or sorbets in. Ice bowls are stunning as a centrepiece for a party table. Ice bowls have to be made in two or three stages and take most of a day to freeze. By six-thirty Friday night, I was able to turn the bowl out and put it in a chilly bin lined with frozen thingies. I called my artwork 'At least you can eat it', and the deal was that I would supply one ice bowl and 2 litres of sorbet or frozen parfait (times two) in the week before Christmas.

The dangerous Mr Greenslade was again in charge of the auction, the bids were flying, the women looked sparkly and glamorous. Men were hooting and egging on the bidders, yet outside The Rocking Frog garden the land is drying up. Farmers are worried, the hills are browning, the low creeks are slowing to a trickle, there is no grass to make hay or silage, there is no market for store lambs, and there is no killing space for old ewes. I do not remember farming being as grim for a long time. But everybody forgot about the grimness last night; even my ice bowl plus ice cream times two attracted multiple bids. I was embarrassed. Richard, our doctor friend of terrier-doping fame, bought it for $100 under instruction from his wife via a telephone bid. I'm not sure that she said he could go as high as $100, though.

This is how you make an ice bowl.

Rose and Berry Ice Bowl

Take a large stainless-steel bowl. Pour an inch of water into the bottom and freeze it. When it is frozen, fit a smaller bowl inside it. I use one with an inch clearance all round. To prevent the inner bowl from floating on the water, weight it down with stones. Arrange roses in the space between the two bowls, I used Bantry Bay, Rhapsody in Blue, and Sexy

Rexy. Pour water into the space up to the level of the roses. The roses need to fit snugly into the space, otherwise they will float to the surface. Freeze again.

When frozen, arrange a circle of berries onto the surface of the ice. I used small strawberries. Later on when the redcurrants are ripe I will use a mixture of redcurrants and strawberries with red roses. Pour enough water in to secure the berries in ice when the water freezes. Freeze. When this layer is frozen, pour water into the space to completely cover the berries, which now cannot float to the surface because they are stuck in the ice. Freeze.

When the last layer is frozen, take the bowl from the freezer, tip the stones out, fill the inner bowl with hot water until it is free, and remove it. Then comes the magic part. Sink the large bowl into a pot of hot water until the ice is free, tip the ice bowl out. And there it stands, a beautiful frozen bowl decorated with roses and berries trapped in translucent ice. 'A miracle of rare device, A sunny pleasure dome with caves of ice.'

Dear Virginia

What can I say! Again I'm astonished by the effort you put into everything you do. With the prognosis for sheep farming looking so dire, you could live well in Wellington, offering expensive evening courses in ice-bowl-making, and truffle-making, and cheese-making. Half the bored bureaucrats here would love to do something useful in their few hours of free evening time before the next day of punishing keyboard-punching.

I'm thinking of making an ice bowl for my cat, with his carefully cut-up meat frozen into it. I could then go away for a weekend knowing the meat would keep for longer. And I'm sure he'd be fascinated, watching his frozen food gradually becoming accessible to him as he licked the ice. Would his tongue stick to it, I wonder?

I have told many people about the ice bowl and all are startled and amazed. I asked the languid ladies of my team at work for their reactions:

'She obviously doesn't have a full-time job.'

'Hasn't she heard of Tupperware?'

'I only learnt to poach an egg two weeks ago.'

The best response was from Jane Waddell. I was sympathizing with her about her broken arm. (On the first night of 'Jack and the Beanstalk', a deeply meaningful Roger Hall panto in which Jane plays the nasty woman, Mrs Stilton, mother of Paris, Jane had to faint backwards into the arms of Paul Jenden. He was . . . er . . . looking the other way and didn't catch her. She fell backwards and broke her arm, then delivered her next line from the floor, got up and played until the end of the show before getting carted off to hospital. When she received her award for best director of the year, she thanked her 'great cast'.) Anyway — where were we? Yes. I asked her if she'd ever made an ice bowl. She replied: 'Is that a sports tournament?'

What happens to the linen tablecloth when the ice bowl melts? Do the redcurrants or strawberries stain the cloth? For a lunch, how long does it last under the hot Canterbury sun? For dinner, what would a candle look like in it after the sorbet had been eaten?

I wish I'd been at the auction. I could do with a Sam, without his big digger, though. I think a trowel is all that he'd need in my garden. It's swirling spring wind right now, and, even though the garden was pristine yesterday, after hours and hours of dead-heading and staking, it's been raining rose petals for twelve hours and the concrete paths look soft and pink, like coconut ice: the melancholy late-spring garden where everything is overblown and just hanging by a thread.

Dear Janice

My strawberries have gone mad with flowers, and the lettuces mad with leaves. We are munching salads, and soon we'll be feasting on lashings of strawberries. Did you ever read *The Flying Postman* when you were little? How I loved that story. It dealt with an abundance of strawberries, a cow, a postman and ice cream.

Yesterday, as we were eating lunch, I saw a monarch butterfly hovering and dancing above the laurel hedge; I was just remarking on its unusual appearance in the garden when a finch swooped upon it and ate it up. Later in the afternoon I heard a deep buzzing roar in the weeping elm. A few minutes later a swarm of bees was clinging to the chimney-pot above Fleur's bedroom. I wondered what they were thinking as they found that a starling had moved into their abandoned hive, or what the starling brood felt as an angry horde of bees retook possession of the chimney. In Nature, always there is death. Something is always making a meal of something else.

As well as the remarkable out-of-territory appearance of the monarch, we have a pair of visiting kereru. They fly low, wooshing overhead at roof-eaves level. Last year, a single bird visited; this year, he has returned with a mate. They sit in the laburnum and eat the leaves. I love them but fear for the health of the laburnums. Kereru look as though they eat a lot. The pukeko hen is hatching a brood down at Kit's pond. Pukekos build their nests in reeds, and they sit perched high in the crown of the reed clump where they have a commanding view of the territory. I have watched the nest ever since the first egg was laid. The hen laid seven eggs. Yesterday when I visited I saw the first chick breaking out of the shell: they have funny pink rubber legs. Harry said he saw a stoat lurking in the orchard, so I wonder how many chicks will survive; they are not like ducklings that can take refuge on the water.

Hope all is well in the garden.

Dear Virginia

It is. In November, while the roses bloom, the soil gives up hidden treasures: Cliff Kidney potatoes. I planted them in August. I surrounded the bed, 6 feet square, with scaffolding planks left over from painting the house about eight years ago. Then, as the shoots emerged, I emptied three compost bins of prime compost into the bed. So the bed was warm and wormy — just as potatoes like it. The Cliff Kidneys thrived and multiplied, unseen. Now the plants have turned yellow and flopped over. I dug up the spuds. Each plant produced about ten to fifteen potatoes, of varying sizes. Some were kidney-sized. (Strange to think that Mr Cliff's kidney has been so memorialized.) They fall from the spade-full of fluffy compost a startling white, softly burnished, like marble. They look as though they have no skin on them.

This is how I make a perfect potato salad. Unlike the ice bowl, I reckon it takes 15 minutes of cooking time and a few minutes of assembly. That's all.

Perfect Potato Salad

Boil the unpeeled potatoes for 6–10 minutes, depending on the size. Don't prick and prod them with a fork while cooking. Don't touch them at all. When they are ready — OK, you can prick one — dump them into a colander to cool. Rush out to the garden — I guess I do everything at a mad pace; you could actually walk slowly out into the garden. Pick some chives, and some mint. If you don't have mint, try sage. It might be flowering right now — beautiful mauve flowers on tall stems standing up from the plant. Are you a gardener or a cook? If you are a gardener, you leave the flowers on the plant because they look lovely. If you are a cook and want more sage leaves, you scissor the flowers off.

If you've picked mint, pile a handful of it onto a chopping board. Sprinkle it with a little sugar. Chop it up. I use an ordinary knife. My mother did, too. Just chop and chop and chop until the board is stained green. But if you are a gadget-collector, you will have in your kitchen a mesalina knife, or maybe 10 mesalinas, that you've been given as presents. Or you may have a grinder, or a blender. Use that. Or a mortar and pestle if you want to be like Jamie Oliver. Whatever you use isn't important. That's culture, not cooking. The point is to bruise, or chop, the herb so the flavours leak out. Then throw this into a big and beautiful bowl. Add a splash of olive oil, a squeezed lemon, some salt and pepper, and a chopped-up red chilli if you like.

If you are going the sage route — heat some oil in a cast-iron frying pan. When it's hot, add sage leaves, a few at a time. Remove with a slotted spoon when they are bright green. Put them on a paper towel until you've done all of them. They will be crisp.

Now, back to the potatoes, which will now be cool enough to peel. I peel them with my fingers. The skins virtually fall off. It's a nice thing to do. Admire the incredibly smooth, shiny surface of the creamy white potato. Slice them uniformly into the big and beautiful bowl with the dressing in it. This is also a lovely thing to do. The potato is so waxy there's no falling apart, no mess. It's a very geometric salad, this. Mix everything up. If you've used sage, add the crisp leaves last. If you want mayonnaise, add it now. And that is it! Perfect.

Serve it with fresh asparagus. I don't grow it. I haven't a big enough garden to have a perennial crop like asparagus. And you need sandy soil. But you can buy it in markets for the next few months, or at the supermarket. For carnivores, add a platter of grilled chicken, steak, or ham off the bone. If you are cooking for a vegetarian, add hard-boiled eggs to the potato salad. If you have to entertain vegans, toss some pinenuts in a pan with a little oil. When the nuts are shiny brown, put them into the salad for non-animal protein.

I've got peas growing, too. Each pod is long and fat and has about ten peas in it. That's a good yield. My strawberry conserve — your recipe — didn't set. I don't know why. I couldn't have simmered it any longer; the strawberries would have fallen apart. Ah, the mysteries of cooking.

Most useful gadget in November: tongs. For picking asparagus spears out of boiling water. That one, the thin one — that's done first! And for taking mussels out of the pot individually, as they open in the steaming broth. Also for picking the smallest Cliff Kidney potatoes out of the saucepan before they overcook.

There is no easy way to say this: I am going to Fiji to stay for a small holiday on Tokoriki, a coral atoll in an island group to the north of Fiji, accessible only by launch and helicopter. I will do nothing but snorkel and sunbathe and swim. My excuse: I'm only going there because Robert is working there.

Hello, Janice

On Thursday, as we stopped at the gate to Bud's Track to scan the hills for sheep, I said, 'Janice is flying to Fiji tomorrow.'

'Why is she going to Fiji?' asked Harry.

'She is going to stay in a *bure* and go swimming and snorkelling and she is going to lie on a beach in the sun.'

'And why would she want to do that? She could have come here for a tailing holiday for nothing.'

I looked at the mountains sprinkled with a light dusting of snow. I felt itchy and cluttered in thick fat clothes and a woolly hat, and thought longingly that Fiji would be rather nice. I growled, 'No I don't think so, Harry.' And I reminded him about our tailing parties.

When we first came to Double Tops, and at odd times since, city friends have expressed a wish to help with the tailing. In our early days we asked a group of friends to a tailing party. We mustered and then we tailed a small mob of Merinos at Tommy's Cabin. After we'd finished we lay under the willow trees and ate a gourmet picnic and drank lots of wine. We thought it a lovely day, but not one of those friends ever mentioned tailing again.

Since then we have twice mustered a tailing party of interested townspeople, with the same result. Tailing is the fastest way I know of to sour people of the country life.

My pig-shooters are the only 'tailers' who return: Luke and Chad Romano and their father, Guy, help us every year. They came yesterday to help tail all the lambs born on the western hill blocks. We had mustered the ewes and their lambs down to the Kirdie's Corner holding paddock over the two preceding days, and on the morning of the tailing Harry and I drove the mob down to temporary yards. Yarding a big mob is a mission, and we always pray we won't have a lamb break. A lamb break is when the lambs at the back of the mob scatter like a shoal of whitebait spooked by a net. Dim-witted lambs leap and bound in all directions with the dogs whooping and barking after them, everybody is shouting and jumping up and down, and the lambs just gaily gallop off into the blue beyond. Yesterday we were lucky and were able to calmly scoop the mob into the pen with the aid of a scrim line.

We tailed 635 lambs from 700 ewes. It took — a while. We stopped for a lunch break of bacon and egg pie — without peas — filled rolls, banana and chocolate cake, and cups of tea. South Islanders make bacon and egg pies with a layer of peas on the bottom. It's soggy and disgusting.

Some of the lambs were large and their tails fat; it reminded me of tailing at home when we were children and the tail bonfires we used to have. Sam Matete was one of the tailing hands, and he always took the fattest tails and the biggest testicles home with him. We were never tempted to eat testicles, but we did try lambs' tails. Lamb-tail bonfires became a spring rite. We would light a fire in the orchard and sit around it in the dark; when the embers were ashen red, we threw the tails into the fire. The wool would flare and singe, and when it had blackened away to nothing the tail inside would be cooked. We would lift the tails from the fire and wait for them to cool a little, then we would peel the skin from the flesh and sprinkle the tails with salt, and sit sucking on the bones. There is not much meat on a lamb's tail, but I remember it with great nostalgia as tasting sweet and burnt and absolutely delicious.

One spring when Kit and Fleur were still malleable, I brought a bag of fat tails home and built a bonfire. With great gusto I told them about tailing at Manutuke and how yummy lambs' tails were, and then I threw the tails onto the embers and inhaled that wonderful smell from childhood. They screwed up their faces at the stink of burning wool. They were disgusted by the charcoal and the grease and the puny strings of meat that were gritty with singed skin and blackened wool. They left me for the warm kitchen and a proper tea. I sat alone by the dying fire, sucking on the bones. I have never burnt lambs' tails again; a spring rite is no fun on your own.

I hope the beach is tropical and the water balmy. Harry says that you will get sunburned and that there will be too much sand. You asked if you could bring me anything from Fiji. I would like the sea.

Dear Virginia

Bill thought I'd catch dengue fever in Fiji. I didn't. It was glorious. Try to get Harry to imagine snorkelling at the reef edge in deep-turquoise, sun-lit water. Maybe tell him it is like mustering multi-hued, swimming sheep.

But now I am back . . . One Monday afternoon, I was

striding through town after a coffee meeting to 'review last week's events with a work colleague' (ie, gossip). My phone rang. It was someone wanting to use my garden for a photo shoot.

'Er — yes,' I said cautiously, not wanting to be the cause of Wellington's creative industries grinding to a halt.

'Tomorrow at 8am,' he said.

I said a lot of ridiculous babble about 'You know how difficult my drive is and maybe they'd prefer not to drive up it.'

'You offering us a challenge?' he asked.

After work I galloped along The Terrace, pushed past slow politicians at the back of Parliament, panted up the hill, rushing home to tidy up. I still hadn't unpacked, and the house was in disarray. A friend's son, who is staying here right now, had to be persuaded to remove his car which was blocking the garden gate.

'Why should I move?' he asked.

He couldn't understand the explanation: filming — big cars.

'So? It's real expensive to park around here,' he moaned.

'Go! Do it!'

Then I called a workmate, Margaret. I see her daily. We've shopped for leaving presents for lucky ex-colleagues together. We've sought support from each other when we've both had times of wishing we were the ones leaving. Margaret knows about the 'look' of things. She has what they call an 'eye'.

'Margaret, what should I do to the sitting room to tidy it up for a film shoot?'

She relished the situation. 'Hmm. You've got a very nice pot in your bedroom, on the chest of drawers. That would look nice in the middle of the coffee table.'

'Right, done!'

I slammed it down, one-handed.

'Why do you keep that jar in the bedroom?'

'I keep my knickers in it.'

A lot of time was wasted while Margaret wheezed with unhelpful laughter. I'm glad I wasn't paying her a life coach's hourly rate for this phone call.

'Now, what shall I do next?'

She just kept laughing.

I crashed the phone down and rushed into the dark garden. I grabbed the washing from the line. Where to put wet washing? Rushed into laundry. Yikes! The washing machine was on. Stephan was doing his washing, mountains of it, on this of all nights. I told him he couldn't hang it out that night. Not allowed. It would ruin the view. I whirled into the kitchen and did the washing-up. I hid the old tea towels in the dishwasher, with an ant-proof jar of white sugar that I didn't think looked very photogenic on the kitchen bench. I swept all the receipts, accounts, invoices, statements, phone numbers, messages about feeding the cat, appointments scribbled on the back of envelopes, all that confetti of tiny bits of paper, off the dining-room table and into the drawer we keep sunglasses in. I piled others on the stairs. Drifts of receipts ended up around the chest of drawers' legs. I pushed them under it, out of sight.

I polished the table. I unfolded a table runner across the table and experimented with different vases with imaginary flowers in them in the middle of the table. The hydrangeas looked too big and bosomy. It would have to be the smaller jug, filled with sweet peas. But I couldn't pick them in the dark. And maybe I couldn't pick them at all, because every single one of them better be blooming its little socks off tomorrow, outside, for the photographer. Did I have the best sweet peas in the world? Probably not.

I went to bed as the wind rose. I set my phone alarm for 5am. I got up about four times in the very short night to do essential things like clean the kitchen windows, pick fluff off the sitting-room carpet, remove the scungy old cushion that's beside the cat door for the convenience of the pampered puss.

Next morning I welcomed the photographer with his black turtleneck and big Hasselblad.

I showed him the garden and suddenly saw it through his eyes: tatty old pantyhose tying up roses, bright-blue plastic string tying up vegetables. Then I left him to it and rushed to work.

'How did it go?' Margaret asked, big-eyed.

'Fine,' I said, then we both fell about laughing. I made her swear she wouldn't tell anyone what we were laughing about. But you never know with Margaret. I've got a suspicion David C knows already. And Tricia.

Dear Janice

Ever since *Common Ground* was published I have been terrified someone might actually want to visit my garden to see if everything I have written about is absolutely true; a photographer would be my worst nightmare. I would need months to tidy up for a shoot, not overnight. I have been truthful, but, as the cliché says, 'beauty is in the eye of the beholder'. I love my garden, but a visitor might think 'What a mess.' On a soft sunny day in spring when you can hear the grass singing and the wind is still, I think of my garden as an oasis of beauty. On a day when the wind rages and the plants are battened down against the wild grey sky, I think my garden is an ugly hole and I despair, I hate the bloody garden; and then when the sun shines again, as it always does, I'm in love again.

Dear Virginia

I know what you mean about the garden's beauty being in the eye of the beholder. Office beauty is another thing entirely. It doesn't exist. Why are offices always so ugly? Post-holiday depression is sinking in. More and more the office seems a disenchanted place. More and more time is spent analysing how we do things instead of actually *doing* things. More meetings get longer and longer, all of them a form of navel-gazing. My intake of stress-relieving licorice and chocolate is getting bigger and bigger. I'm increasingly seeing myself as a child, with a child's dependence and lack of freedom. The office is the mother, with the mother's inability to see that her child is capable of more.

I must get out, into the sunshine of a very different kind of life, where the grass occasionally sings. I see my going into the garden as a metaphor for leaving work. I am hungry for risk. I don't want life handed me on a plate, complete with sick leave and four weeks' annual leave in return for agreeing to all company policies. All this spreadsheeting and writing reports about projects completed moons ago — I can't do it anymore. Do you become more impatient the older you get? I do. I think offices are for young, ambitious people. And I've lost that ambition.

Every day at the desk is another day I witness the murder

of the English language. Apart from flowers, family and food, I love my language and want to pull out the weeds that keep growing in it. I've spent this week having meetings in order to set things called 'smart goals'. Someone has just emailed me: 'Are your smart goals in your ball park yet?'

PS: The little dairy down below the office building has upped its sale of chocolate fish to 375 a week. We live in stressful times.

Dear Janice

Does the little dairy publish a weekly chocolate-fish sales report as an indicator of public servant distress, like a Colmar Brunton poll?

December

Dear Janice

The calf marking is over, and during the course of it we found Pumpkin a new friend, a small orphan calf we have christened Buttercup. She is a golden Charolais. Poor Zucchini the lamb has been rather cast aside by Pumpkin. This week Harry is breaking in a very large and friendly piebald horse called Cruise to take on a horse trek over the mountains on Mount Whitnow with the 'last of the real men'.

Do you remember me writing that I covet a glass-house but that I'm afraid to buy one in case it means our retirement will be at Double Tops on account of filling my retirement criteria of a place where I can grow tomatoes? Well, I don't know what made me do it, but yesterday I drove in to town and bought one. It is a Juliana, a Danish greenhouse, it is made of polycarbonate, not glass, and reported to be easy to assemble; not that there is any great need to assemble it in a hurry because it's December. The frost season is over. The glass-house is probably an unwise move. I'll be marooned here now until Harry is carried out as a stiff in a wooden box.

The sky hangs grey and heavy, but no matter how we beseech it, it will not rain.

Dear Virginia

I am delighted about the glass-house.

What is a 'real man'? Today I worked with Jerome Leota at the recording studio. Jerome told me about his wife, Rachel's, full-on job in the Corrections Department. 'So I do the shopping and cooking.' Ah, ha. A young house-husband? No. He's an early-childhood teacher at the Newtown Community Centre crèche. He finishes work before Rachel does, so he does the domestic stuff. I haven't hired him because of his cooking skills. I've hired him to put some cool Pacific vocals down on two song tracks. So — I think there are more 'real men' out there than Harry supposes, just a different sort of real man, perhaps.

Like you, we have had no rain. But, unlike you, we can sip our lattes, or our bottled water, and be (temporarily) unaffected by the drought. Jane and I went for a walk worthy of your mustering on Sunday, and ended up sitting on top of Belmont trig (height 475m). The grass was brown. The sheep appeared to have no water at all other than a muddy scoop in the ground, in full sun, that had shrunk to the size of a hand basin, and was a deep bilious-green slime. I hope Buttercup has better water than that. I told Jane that I wanted to pour my bottle of spring-fed glacier-pure water into the pond to help the animals out. She told me I was being ridiculous, which of course I was. But there is something mad about a world where you can walk up a dust-dry hill carrying a bottle of glacier-melt water that you bought at the supermarket.

Good morning, Janice

I could scream, have a tantrum, take all my clothes off in the garden, even cut my throat — and not a blind bit of difference would it make. The garden was frozen at six this morning. A frost on December 8th is the equivalent of being shot in a sanctuary. The garden should be safe by December the 8th. It wasn't.

Yesterday, my boys, Harry, Jason the bricklayer from Sydney, and Hamish the Lincoln student, spent all day assembling my little glass-house. It's not quite finished, so I did not put my ten beautiful heritage tomato plants inside it. Also outside were courgettes, a cucumber and an aubergine in the seed bed. In the garden itself, I had a row of sweet corn and two rows of Jersey Benne potatoes in flower. All are frosted to their degrees of tolerance, their beauty ruined. A row of burnt potatoes is an ugly thing. The courgettes are totally munted, and the tomatoes severely stunted.

The frost is a major tragedy for me, but Harry, already in 'real man' mode, gives me a look that says 'For goodness sakes, woman, what the hell are you on about?' and goes on eating his breakfast. I'm devastated and say that at least he might be sympathetic, and he says, 'Plants grow again — plant some more' and he asks if the tulips are all right! Well, as you know, tulips have long since disappeared underground until next spring. I think he means the irises, how little he knows about gardens! He's gone down to the stables to ready his horse for the big ride.

Les, another real man, rings. I ask him if there was a frost in

Hawarden. 'Oh yes,' he says, 'I've been out hosing. You get up early and hose.' And I know that he was probably up at four and I'm just a sluggard! Real men are men like the man in the Speight's beer advertisement, laconic, tough and silent, they sit astride rough horses with ease, their stoic faces shaded by dark-brimmed hats. Real men ride off into the hills eschewing the world of women — until they return and need their dirty clothes washed and their meals cooked.

I look at the photo of you reading languidly beneath your rose-strewn pergola, with, no doubt, three-feet-high tomatoes just out of view, and I cry 'Unfair, unjust'; and I lament these bitter hills and then I get a grip. The sun is shining and the tomatoes will grow again. They will just be late.

> The Moving Finger writes; and, having writ,
> Moves on: nor all your Piety nor Wit
> Shall lure it back to cancel half a Line,
> Nor all your Tears wash out a Word of it.

Omar Khayam was a wise man. You cannot change what has been. Move on. Do not look back. I am looking forward to using my lovely little greenhouse.

Dear Virginia

I am very sorry about that frost. Will you still have time to plant more tomatoes and courgettes? I hope so. I am envious of your glass-house. You will grow big red tomatoes this year and you will quickly forget this frost.

Imagine what settlers felt when their precious plants, brought with them or obtained with difficulty here, met the same fate. It's so hard for us to imagine the value of plants then. The rose from Mother's garden — the mother you know you will never see again after leaving England, the potatoes you brought all the way from home because they are the ones that have sustained you for generations. And then the frost comes.

Tell me how you roast a lamb.

Dear Janice

I shall begin at the beginning, which is the lamb hanging on the hooks in the killing shed — you asked for it! Be assured that the Double Tops, free-range, hill-country, mixed-herbage-fed lamb hanging on the hooks is the best there is.

Dealing to the carcass: the lamb is hanging by its hind legs, so take a meat saw and saw the lamb in half; this is not as easy as it sounds because you have to keep the saw very straight so the carcass is cleaved evenly in two. 'Cleaved' is a good word, an experienced butcher takes a heavy cleaver and chops the lamb in two in a very few strokes. Now take half the lamb and cut off the hind quarter — the butcher who taught us lamb cuts told us to leave the last loin chop on the leg to stop the leg drying out when roasted. Cut off the shank. Now you have the loin chops, which you separate from the rib chops which form a rack of lamb. You count seven ribs and cut the rack off there; what is left is the forequarter, which you can separate into a shoulder roast and neck chops, or you can bone the whole quarter into a butterflied shoulder for the barbeque. When you have dealt to the other half of the lamb, you will have all those cuts plus four shanks. If you want to get technical, you can then gourmet-cut the leg into cuts like lamb straps and rump roasts. I like to roast a leg whole or bone it out to a butterflied-leg barbeque cut. In *The Forsyte Saga*, the Soames Forsytes used to have a roast saddle of lamb on Sundays. Remember? A saddle of lamb is both sides of the loin area unhalved. Saddle is a delicious roast, but very extravagant as you use nearly all the chops at once.

Right, so we have the leg roast, or a forequarter. The forequarter meat is yummier and sweeter, but it is fattier. If you have a fetish about fat, roast a leg.

Roast Lamb

I pre-heat the oven to 200 degrees. If you are going to do this, make sure the oven is clean, otherwise the kitchen will fill with smoke. I put the lamb in a covered roasting dish, sometimes alone, sometimes dressed with rosemary and garlic, depending on what vegetables I'm going to serve. For a farmhouse roast with mint sauce, peas, carrots and new potatoes, the lamb should be undressed.

I leave the leg in at 200 for about half an hour until the skin is browned, then I turn the oven down to 150 and leave it there for 2 or 3 hours. It doesn't matter how long exactly. If you are cooking until 'meat off the bone fall', you cannot cook the joint for too long. Slow-cooked lamb is a good dinner-party feast for city visitors: one, because most city people do not cook roasts; and, two, because you do not have to worry about taking the meat out at just the right time and resting it.

When I serve meals I never plate up — except for the shearers and to display entrée designer desserts. My mother always said you should let people be responsible for how much they eat by letting them serve themselves. She said it was an arrogance to decide how much a person should have on their plate.

I serve all the vegetables in very hot dishes, and the roast is on a very hot carving dish. There is nothing worse than a lukewarm roast with congealing fat. Yuk. The dishes are all put in the middle of the table and garnished with handfuls of mint and parsley from the garden, and there is light gravy and mint sauce and pepper and salt, and all the individual plates are very hot and it is all very yum. I suppose it sounds very 1960s.

It is cold today, and dry, but earlier in the week we had 15ml of rain, a small blessing. The clover will be happy.

Dear Virginia

Rarely do I roast a leg of lamb. Even for nephew nights, my regular dinners for growing boys, my roasts will be chickens rather than lambs. I haven't written about nephew nights, but you can imagine them: we have had curries, pies, stews, pastas, meatballs, etc, and large puddings. I am an expert on feeding young men aged between seventeen and thirty-five.

Imagine my astonishment when I had a meeting with an ethereal young project manager last week who told me she's researching for SPARC. She has to find out what teenage boys eat. I asked her what she'd discovered. 'Weetbix, pies and potatoes,' she said. I didn't ask her how long it had taken her to find this out. Maybe I could become an expensive Ministry of Health consultant on teenage boys' diets?

A difference between city and country cooking is that we urban dwellers use mince as a staple meat. We don't go in for large cuts of meat that look like recognizable body parts. We like deconstructed meat. We go for Wiener schnitzel (already crumbed) sausages, stir-fry meat (already cut up). Steaks or chops, sitting in neat rows under plastic. Even our stewing meat is pre-cut.

I can trace my life history through mince. First, when I was a child, I remember helping my mother mince up the leftover lamb from the Sunday roast for shepherd's pie for Monday's tea. The minced meat was mixed with leftover gravy and onions, put in a loaf-shaped dish and topped with a cloud of the softest, butteriest mashed potato. I always got the job of raking the top with a fork to make patterns that crisped up nicely in the oven. Now shepherd's pie is invariably made with beef mince. The English always add Worcester sauce.

When Boyd and I lived in California, newly married and newly recipe-booked, we bought *The Joy of Cooking,* the American cook's bible, and tried to eat like Americans. So mince became meat loaf. It's a wonderfully dense loaf of highly-seasoned meat held together with eggs, topped with tomato sauce. It is the best leftover ever. A slice of meat loaf between two slices of bread — now that would be a perfect lunchtime sandwich when you are mustering or dipping. You would need a siesta afterwards so you could digest it.

I use mince like play-dough. I love making meatballs which we eat with pasta. Meatballs and a tomato sauce and pasta is a much nicer dish than the NZ staple spag bol where everything is mixed into one big slop.

Here is a tip for using mince. When browning mince, never

use it straight from the fridge. Let it reach room temperature on the bench. If it is too cold when it hits the hot fat, it bleeds instead of sears.

I feel the new year fast approaching. Just as your glass-house will signal the beginning of a basil- and aubergine-growing experiment at Double Tops (!), I feel the new year will be the precursor of a different way of life on my city terrace. So I'm thinking about your roast lamb and thinking of my own need to slow down, and smell the baking.

Dear Janice

A week after I last wrote, the glass-house was wasted by wind, strewn about the lawn, bent and scratched.

The salesman had said it would take two men about four hours to put together. Harry decided it would be a project for Jason the bricklayer. He asked Jason if he thought he could manage it. Jason said, 'Yeah, no worries.' Hamish, the holiday student worker, was co-opted to help. I was not assigned a role.

The glass-house assembly was a classic case of 'systemic failure' right there in my own kitchen garden. How easy it was to watch yet be unaware of the farrago going on. This is what happened. Jason looked at the plans, got the general idea, but didn't read the plans from A to Z. Harry didn't ask Jason if he'd read the plans. He just assumed he had. If you take the word 'assume' you get ass — u — and me. The danger in assuming anything is that it can make an 'ass out of you and me'. An hour after the work began, I strolled out and asked how the polycarbonate sheeting was to fit into the metal framework which was standing on the lawn like an undressed glass-house. 'Ah,' said Jason. The framework was disassembled and the project resumed from the bottom up. At the end of the day a nice little glass-house stood in the garden. How excited I was; only the door was to be put on. Harry went away riding his newly broken horse, Cruise, up the rock ridges of the Puketerakis with the 'last of the real men'. The wind didn't blow and the wee glass-house shone in the sun.

Monday morning, Jason finished the door and packed up. I went out for an inspection. I found a large bundle of black plastic mouldings left over. 'What are these for?'

'Buggered if I know, but I don't think they are important,' said Jason.

I thought they must be important so I measured them, then I measured the base of the glass-house, and then I looked carefully. The black plastic mouldings should have been inserted right at the beginning of the assembly; they held the plastic sheets rigid and connected them to the base. 'It will have to be taken apart and begun again,' I said. I went back inside and began thinking, as one does when things go wrong, about project management. And quite suddenly I saw why or how the reinforcing rods and the bolts that were meant to connect the platform to the concrete foundations were never used on the Cave Creek platform project. My glass-house black plastic bits were the platform reinforcing rods and bolts. They were not used because nobody came along and asked, 'What are these for?' Or maybe they did, and the reply was 'Buggered if I know.' I began to hate the glass-house, just a little.

The project was begun again, from the beginning, but the frames were bent and some of the screws were broken. We were busy weaning and dipping lambs. Jason and Hamish were planning to be away for the weekend. The glass-house wasn't finished by Friday. On Saturday night a nor'wester brewed, and by morning the wind was screeching in the trees. The little glass-house lay in tatters about the lawn. Systemic failure had wrecked my dream. At least it was only a glass-house. I ordered it removed from where I could ever see it again. Harry slunk off and got the tip truck and away went the dream, I hoped, to the dump.

Later I found the pieces carefully packed in bundles in a shed. I rang Mrs Ewart and offered her a free glass-house, as is, where is. Her husband, David, is a clever handyman in his spare time. I was sure he could resurrect the glass-house so that she could grow tomatoes for her 'tray of twelve'. (Remember the tray of twelve? The premier class in the vegetable section at the A&P show.) When I told Harry I had given the glass-house away, our marriage was very nearly over, and I had to retract the offer.

Dear Virginia

Marital bliss is too precious to let it suffer from the systemic failure of a glass-house assembly. My brother fixed my draughty front door. He nailed draught-proofing strips all around the doorjamb and door, the result being that now we can no longer shut the front door. But, hey, it isn't worth falling out over such domestic calamities. The 'moving finger' has already moved on. I wonder if the 'last of the real men' ever got to hear Harry tell the sorry glass-house tale, in an isolated hut one dark night on Mount Whitnow. Cheer up!

Here's something to amuse you. Remember the Dairy Board CD-ROM we are making? Rachel was test-running it on her computer. Kirsty was on the phone a few metres from Rachel's desk, trying to negotiate a tricky deal with a client. Suddenly the air was filled with loud mooing (bad) and farting (worse) noises. Kirsty had to explain to her client that she wasn't in a cowshed, on her mobile. She was actually at work, in our office, where her pod-mate was test-driving a CD-ROM. It just didn't sound credible.

Christmas is coming to the office. At lunchtime today the Salvation Army band was playing carols in Lambton Quay, the sun glinting off the trumpets. Those who work the last day before Christmas in our company get to have Christmas mince pies and a Secret Santa with their last morning tea. Our team always buys Pandoro mince pies. Secret Santas are an office convention where everyone draws straws to decide who they buy a $10 or less present for. So each person gets a gift from an anonymous donor. Some gifts are well thought-out to suit the receiver. Some come complete with poems, paeons of praise. But there's always some poor person who gets something like a shower cap in a box from a hotel bathroom, or a packet of Cheezels.

Christmas is reason enough for office staff to get creative with staplers, hole punches and packs of coloured paper. Snow crystals can be made from hole-punched manila folders. Deadly weapons like the paper cutter and the gun staplers are in high demand for making and hanging paper chains. Unfortunately kids appear in the office, released from school, wanting to go Christmas shopping, whiling away the time playing on the computers, xeroxing their faces and blowing prints up to A3 size in the printer room. I say 'unfortunately' because there's always one adventurous one who will play with the staple-gun.

(Oh, Health and Safety Officer: quake in your little black shoes!) When I was working at Capital Radio in London, and Robert was four, I had to rush him to hospital because he'd staple-gunned his thumb. The doctor said it was 'a seasonal hazard'.

The lopped-off top of a pinus radiata appeared overnight and was put in the biggest rubbish bin, the one by the photocopier. The IT guys stabilized it with phone books and old diaries. A couple of not-so-busy secretaries (sorry: personal assistants) decorated the tree with a thousand paper cranes they'd folded last week out of memo pads. Raewyn peeled the plastic bottoms off all the hole punches and showered the tree with the paper holes; office snow, she called it.

We are all waiting now for the last working day of the year, and the mince pies and the Secret Santa. Then we can go home and be grown-ups.

Dear Janice

The day the glass-house dream was shattered was the Road Party day. After showering, dressing and a reconciliation brew of strong coffee, Harry and I drove up the road to Haydon Downs, very slowly, with one large platter of cheesy walnut biscuits and another of brandy-snap cones filled with cream. We arrived early to help Heather and Barry. They have not lived on the Virginia Road for long, and there were families they had not met.

We hold a road party once a year, because it is very important to know your neighbours when you live on a country road to nowhere. Things happen: accidents, snowstorms, droughts, scrub fires, births, deaths; it is easier to ask the neighbours for help if you know them. Everybody who lives and works on the road is invited to the party, everybody comes. This year it was lunch, some years it's dinner. We drank champagne, we talked, we ate lots of food. Energetic people played tennis, the children swam in the pool, we ate more food and talked and drank more wine. Heather made coffee and brought out Christmas cake and mince pies; there was a treasure hunt, and suddenly it was five o'clock and families began to drift home, calling out 'Merry Christmas' as they went. The Road Party heralds Christmas on the Virginia Road. I got that pre-Christmas sick feeling — so much to do, so little time.

A piece of advice on filling brandy snaps. You must have a piping bag and a few fluted nozzles. Once you have owned a piping bag you would never be without one. They are useful for filling things with cream, making very professional-looking meringues and éclairs and for icing cakes.

Dear Virginia

I have never used a piping bag. I fear I would never make it as a country cook.

On that last working afternoon, Cathy changed the staff room into a party place. A box for beer caps and ring pulls, a rubbish bin under each dripping wine cask. Tina stood on a table using typist's white-out to paint the bottoms of the fluorescent tubes as the office doesn't have dimmer switches. She had raided the stationery cupboard and had twenty-three bottles of the stuff at her feet. All very last-minute: a centrepiece of pine cones and pohutukawa blossoms with floppy pink petunias stuck in the top arrived from Customer Services.

Cheezels, crackers, chippies, sausage rolls and salted peanuts were laid out. Oh, the salt! Everyone waited until the CEO had told us what a great bunch of hard-working people we were and how she hoped we all had a great holiday and would work even harder next year.

We had a wine or a beer or two. By 6pm everyone who was single and without children had moved on to the pub. Everyone else was on the road or in their train, thinking of everything they had to do between now and Christmas morning.

Dear Janice

The inspirational stories this festive season are about sheep. In the spring when the lambs were very small, Cap, one of Harry's heading dogs, got loose somehow and spent a 'fun' afternoon worrying a lamb in the front paddock. When I was feeding my pets I noticed this poor little lamb all hunched over, I picked her up and found all her belly skin ripped off. There was also a huge gap down the inside of her thigh where the skin had torn away from the muscle, it was a horrible injury. I'm sure any vet would have said she had to be 'euthanized' but I've watched the animal world for a long time and seen the tremendous desire to live, the huge drive to survive injury at all costs, so I thought I'd better save this lamb. I caught her twice a day and squeezed Savlon cream down the gap between skin and muscle; the wound stank and festered. In the old days when we had access to penicillin I would have given her a shot and all would have been well, but we cannot buy it anymore and to get it from the vet is more complicated than applying for a passport. The lamb's hold on life was fragile for a week or so, then came the morning I couldn't catch her and I knew she would survive. She is going to join the pet flock. She is a special sheep and deserves a long and happy life.

Dear Virginia

I cannot come up with inspirational stories about lambs this Christmas. But I did have one tiny inspirational moment. It happened today. Well, for me it was actually a huge, earth-shattering moment, but if you'd been walking through the office during that moment you probably wouldn't have noticed anything out of the ordinary. Just before the mince pies and Secret Santa morning tea today, I got an email that so uninspired me that it inspired me, if you see what I mean. It said, in part: *Project managers will be working to critique and analyse their communications in order to strengthen their effectiveness around improving practice. Also looking at the first cut of the data from the sustainability focus group on cohorts who have exited the project.*

I looked at it. My heart ached. My stomach rumbled. I wanted to take my Pandoro mince pie and go home, sit under the roses, beside the star jasmine, and eat it with a large whisky. I wanted my friends from the office to be there, too, in the sunshine. And I wanted to share emails with people who spoke the same language as I do: plain English. All I could understand from that last email of the year was: *cohorts who have exited the project.* It was a sign.

I reached for a piece of A4 paper and, in that earth-shattering moment, wrote my resignation letter.

Dear Janice

Congratulations on exiting the project. Do you think your future will be sustainable? Merry Christmas.

Dear Virginia

Christmas is over. I never have time to write letters in Christmas week. Our family scattered to various locations and occupations this Christmas. Howard and Gin went fishing. Rowan and Wayne went to their piece of bush out the back of Masterton. Hugh and Co went to their railway carriages. So we had a family dinner before the Big Day. When we were decorating the tree, I noticed that the directions on the back of a box of 100 musical Christmas lights said: *How to avoid exploding lambs this Xmas. Care should be taken to ensure that lambs are not used in positions where they may contact combustible materials or material likely to melt.* Another little detail that I thought would make you smile: the box was bought at Farmers.

Happy After-Christmas from Wellington's exploding lambs to Double Tops' inspirational ones.

Dear Janice

Between late November and Christmas week I picked bucket-loads of strawberries, so of course strawberries were on the December menu. Strawberry ice cream, cassis-macerated strawberries, strawberry *mille-feuilles*, strawberry pancakes, strawberry conserve. I didn't cook a Christmas dinner. It wasn't my turn. But every year we host a Boxing Day lunch.

It is hard to find playwrights, artists, singers, famous writers and eccentrics out in the hills, so on Boxing Day we always ask the entire, slightly eccentric, McCubbin-Howell family whose children are potentially famous, and their dog Flossie, who is suspected of taking performance-enhancing drugs, plus all my family.

The Boxing Day menu never changes, it's a tradition and, as New Zealand is short of traditions, I keep lunch the same every year; well, not quite, but the skeleton is the same. We begin with nibbles. This year we ate fresh roasted nuts, figs, muscatels and olives and little spring rolls made with pork and with cabbage and coriander from the garden. The main is always a warm glazed ham with new potatoes and many sprigs of mint, fresh garden peas, green salad, a red salad, a round of *brie* and home-made bread rolls. This year the green salad was lettuce and rocket with basil, Kalamata olives and tomatoes. There was no red salad, but stuffed eggs instead. The idea for eggs came from a Russian Christmas menu in *Cuisine*. I made the eggs as Mother used to make them; they looked pretty, bright-yellow mashed yolks with green capers. The green peas were a tad sparse in the garden on account of a sparrow attack, so I combined them with small broad beans and made a warm salad of peas, beans, chopped mint and feta.

The main is always followed by strawberry ice cream and blackcurrant sorbet accompanied by strawberries and raspberries, baby meringues and whipped cream. Christmas is such an indulgence, but not for Fleur who is in perpetual training for body-trashing races like the Coast to Coast. After a light meal she went off for a long run while the rest of us finished off lolling around drinking coffee and eating Bailey's Irish Cream chocolates.

Ice cream is not difficult to make, and you do not need an ice-cream-maker if you make a recipe that uses beaten eggs and whipped cream. The ice creams that need an ice-cream machine are the traditional custard-based ice creams made with eggs and unbeaten cream. These need to be beaten, as they freeze to break up the ice crystals and aerate the mix. Sorbets are better made in a machine, too. I will give you an easy ice cream recipe which is based on one I got from Michael Lee Richards when my friend Alison and I were kitchen assistants at one of his cooking demonstrations.

Strawberry Ice Cream

1kg strawberries
500g sugar
½ cup water
6 egg whites
500ml cream

Try to buy jam strawberries, they taste better than the designer sort. Slowly simmer the strawberries until they are soft and watery, then strain through a sieve — leave the juice to cool.

Put the sugar and ½ cup of water in a copper-bottomed saucepan, bring to the boil and then leave boiling for 6 minutes. While the sugar and water is boiling, beat the egg whites until soft. After the sugar syrup has boiled for 6 minutes pour it straight into the egg whites — beating all the time. Beat until the mixture is very stiff. Cool, this can be hastened by putting the bowl in the deep-freeze.

When the mixture is cool, beat the cream, fold the strawberry juice into the whipped cream, and then fold the meringue mixture in to the cream mixture. If you are going to serve the ice cream in scoops, pour it into a clean ice-cream container and freeze. If you want to serve the ice cream more decoratively, freeze it in a ring mould. Unless the ring mould is plastic, the ice cream should be removed from the mould as soon as it is frozen and stored in cling-film.

You will now be left with 6 egg yolks, which you could use to make a *quiche Lorraine*, which is traditionally made with onions, bacon, cheese, egg yolks and cream. A very intense rich quiche, not high and 'pouffy' like the big fat quiches you buy in cafés; or you could use the egg yolks to make a rich French vanilla ice cream.

Six-egg-yolks Vanilla Ice Cream
2 cups cream
1 cup milk
1 cup sugar
6 egg yolks
2 tsp vanilla

Beat the egg yolks and the sugar in a heavy-bottomed saucepan until they are creamy. In another saucepan, heat the milk and cream until they are almost boiling, then pour onto the egg-yolk mixture, stirring all the time. Put this saucepan over a very low heat and stir with a wooden spatula until the mixture thickens and coats the spatula. Do not boil or the eggs will scramble. Stir in the vanilla, or you could add a liqueur like Kahlua.

When the custard is cold, pour it into an ice-cream machine and churn. If you do not have a machine, you can freeze the custard in a bowl and then take it out when almost frozen and give it a spin in a food processor before re-freezing.

All the berries in the ice cream are from the garden, the eggs are from Barry and Heather up the road. We barter eggs for mutton, but the milk and cream are from the shop. It would be too much to milk a cow. You have to be a special sort of person to milk a cow. Mandy and Dugald next door keep a house cow. Dugald likes milking the cow in the morning, it's his thinking time. I have been hen-less ever since a ferret wantonly killed them. Ferrets are like humans, they kill for the pleasure of killing, far more than they can ever eat. I miss keeping hens and I miss their inquiring conversations. I am thinking of re-establishing the hens with a rooster who I hope will chase the pukekos out of the orchard. The pukeko family on Kit's pond are getting hungry. I like pukekos but, now their territory has dried off, they are eyeing the garden and I'm wondering if their residency is such a wonderful idea.

January

Dear Janice

Happy New Year from everyone at Double Tops.

The Virginia Road sleeps from Christmas Day until the second of January. The dust lies still between the gravelstones and the grass verges dry brown in the sun, the Pretty Bend rise shimmers in the heat. Terry of the Haydon Downs cottage is on holiday; Barry and Heather are gardening in Blenheim; and motorcycle Keith is not rattling past, on his way to work in Kaipoi. These are our daily commuters, all grounded elsewhere. No stock agents, land agents or fertilizer reps call. There are no stock trucks thundering down the road, no fertilizer trucks, no school bus, no farmers checking their down-country pastures. The road sleeps. Tomorrow, January third, rural New Zealand will awaken, the dust will rise in great swirling clouds as the trucks and cars roar past in the wheel tracks, belting hither and thither in the elusive pursuit of national productivity and GDP.

Dear Virginia

In that first week back at the office in the new year, everyone dreams of change. We are all glad to see each other. We all chat a lot more than usual, ask 'Where did you go?' and listen to long answers. If I see a cluster of more than three colleagues gathered around a computer screen it isn't because they're studying the annual report or their timesheets. It's holiday photos, or an exciting new site on the Internet. Many colleagues have files of their dream real-estate on screen. 'Look at this one. We were just driving past and—' We all scratch our sunburn, look at the rural dream — 10 acres — and say 'Aw! Fantastic!' And we think 'I wish', because buried inside the soul of every urban office worker is a longing for a couple of acres of prime rural land.

Health and Safety is back with renewed vigour, generating fresh and dire warmings: *The muscles you use for computing will have relaxed over the holidays and could be easily damaged if you throw yourself at your computer willy nilly. Take mini breaks and* *micro pauses. Read the ergonomic exercises in our H and S folder.* After a macro pause — a coffee break — another Eeyore prediction of gloom pings into the inbox: *Make sure your personal earthquake kit is up to date. Include fresh water, torch, tin opener, warm clothes, cans of food. Re-familiarize yourself with the position of the Civil Defence kit in the goods lift stairwell.*

But it's water off a duck's back for me. I have the beginning of my new life. I've handed in my notice! My last day is in February — so soon. No more evenings of worry, peanuts, licorice, and chocolate. I shall arise from the ashes of my past life, and try to do all the things that have been on my life's To Do list for thirty years.

Dear Janice

My glass-house, which I shall call the Phoenix, has arisen from its ashes and now stands glistening in the vegetable garden. It's beautiful. I can gaze at it from the kitchen window. It has a high peaked roof to shed snow, a little sliding door, and an automatic window in the roof which mysteriously opens and closes as the temperatures alter.

Last week Harry and Jason spent a whole day putting it up. Getting the last pieces to lock together was tricky as some of the struts were bent after the disaster, but eventually, and with me bracing the house from the rear, they clicked it all into place, like sliding the last piece of a jigsaw puzzle into its slot. With all the black plastic foot-pieces, the construction is as firm and tight as a winter cabbage and will withstand the strongest winds, I'm sure. Our marriage has survived. Harry would never jettison me. He'd never be able to find his underpants.

Dear Virginia

Inspired by the resurrection of the glass-house, tonight I am making your strawberry conserve from *Common Ground* again! If at first you don't succeed . . .

Last night I picked new, tender (but well over a foot long) scarlet runners and made my first summer meal! I have had a stream of visitors all January — mostly from Auckland — and all they want to do is lounge around in cafés. I have become allergic to cafés. On Saturday I was in La Bella Italia from 11.30am until 4.40pm!! My new resolution is to NOT eat out.

Not until the vegetables have stopped producing. My life will change totally. The amount of disposable income Auckland and Wellington people spend in cafés is HUGE. As an antidote, yesterday we walked the ridge above Eastbourne — a good four-hour walk.

Hello Janice

When I am a very old lady and an earnest historian asks me what summer was like on the farm in the olden days when there were farms, I will mumble, 'Heat and dust, heat and dust.' And then I will mutter, 'Salad.'

The summer heat shimmers in the hills. It smells of dry tussock and baking gravelstones, of thistledown and river-bed gorse flowers simmering under a hot blue sky and a yellow sun. And the dust? The dust smells of warm road-gravel laced with sheep excrement and diesel; it swirls in billowing white clouds behind rumbling, rattling stock trucks. It smells of powdered sheep-yard dirt and greasy wool and fetid dags. Sheep-yard dust clogs your nostrils with brown gunge and stinks in your hair. In the evening the dust dances with sandflies against the slow glow of the sinking sun behind the dark hills. Dusk is dipping time, and the smell of the dip machine and the fumes of the little motor that drives it are blended with the damp of wet wool and the pitiful bleating of lambs crying for their mothers and the harsh barking of yard dogs; these are the smells and sounds of January.

Salad. I will remember salad because it is our staple diet in January. It is late by the time we get in from weaning and dipping, I'm usually tired, and there is a student to cook for as well as Harry and me. Students must be like your nephews. They like lots of meat and potatoes and peas. I tack a salad onto this for the Lincoln University student. The January evening meal goes something like this. Dig new potatoes, place in a pot of boiling, salted water with a handful of mint. Later, put a pot of minted salted water (whoops, no salt for us!) on for the Wattie's frozen peas, light the barbecue ready to sear lamb chops, lamb steaks or lamb kebabs. In between setting the table and preparing the vegetables, I make a salad.

Salads are only limited by your imagination. I take lettuce from the garden, usually iceberg lettuce mixed with designer lettuce and rocket or mesclun mix. I spread the lettuce mix on a platter and then add the extras. Cucumber, basil leaves, tomatoes, feta, olives, roasted walnuts, crunchy bacon, *croûtons*, boiled egg, capers, fennel, shaved Parmesan, blue cheese. Not all together of course, but in combinations. Tomatoes, cucumber, basil, feta and olives go well. Bacon, blue cheese and walnuts are another good combo. Salad is easy.

January was very hot and very dry. The hill creeks slowed to a trickle and some died. The river below the wool shed dried to a bed of white-rimed stones. The lawns burned crisp beneath the hot blue sky. I couldn't water the roses, and they sickened in the dry heat. The humidity was often under 40%, which is anathema to roses, and they curled their petals inwards. The sparrows were so hungry they ate the new rose-bush leaves.

I do not entertain many visitors in January, apart from the shearers, and I'm not sure that shearing catering comes into the realm of entertaining. I have a confession: I cheated with the sponges this year. I didn't make William Taylor's sponge. I bought Ernest Adams sponge slabs and spread them with raspberry jam and whipped cream, I decorated them with a pile of very ripe raspberries from the garden and dusted the creation with icing sugar. Very simple, very good and very 'fifties. That sort of culinary creation decorated the *Women's Weekly* summer cover once upon a time when sponge-making prowess was an admirable attribute for a woman to have.

Dear Virginia

Now that I've resigned, everything that was drear and depressing is now humorous and even stimulating. Emails ping-pong back and forth about the new office obsession — goal-setting — and I just smile. This sort of thing: *Tena koe. Goals are deeply contextualized in your practice and are built from evidence of current work, recognizing what you have built on and where knowledgeable others may be needed . . .* It went on for pages, but I had no need to read further, and much less need to pretend to understand it.

I'm in what they call here 'a good space'. I will celebrate with a lemon tart from Smith's the Grocer.

Good afternoon, Janice

We mustered two hill blocks early this morning. We began before sun-up, but actually the sun never did get up, it remained completely hidden by cloud. A good morning to muster. Lambs dipping and dagging are being done this week, and I'm making ice creams and sorbets for a friend's son's twenty-first dinner for sixty (remember the ice-bowl-and-sorbet art auction contract?). Tomorrow two Danish couples arrive to stay, and the garden is dry and needs constant water and the berries need picking, and the day has all gone awry because I didn't have essential goals contextualized into my work plan, neither are there any knowledgeable others to monitor my programme and suggest I improve my behaviours. I can see quite clearly, after reading your goals, that I need to have a plan. Not one that is written in understandable terms, but a gobbledegook one so that no one will really know whether I've achieved all the stated goals and key performance indicators or not.

I found the goal-setting part of your beginning-of-the-year letter just cause for resignation, and also deeply depressing. In our sector of the economy there is little time for detailed goal-setting. Daily goals are often derailed by nature. The plan is to set out at 8am to muster a block, estimated time to complete the job three hours, arrive back 11am, one hour spraying weeds, lunch. 1pm gardening until 5pm for me, fencing for Harry. At five it's time to check troughs again, feed dogs, get washing in, get dinner ready.

And this is what happens. Steers have wrecked the trough. One hour delay to muster start. Drive out to muster, pigs have knocked down the Taranaki gate or shooters have left a gate open. Sheep are spread over three blocks. Muster takes five hours as sun is hot and sheep are hiding in shade. Lunch is late, 2pm maybe. Spraying is abandoned. The fencing job is urgent. It takes until 6pm. I know that Harry and Hamish won't be in until after six, so I see an opportunity to squeeze in an extra job and go off to do some weed spraying of my own. Return at six-thirty. Still have to feed dogs, get washing in. Dinner prep is very late. Hamish comes in at seven. I have to give him a beer because dinner isn't ready. The whole day feels out of control. Plans have not been adhered to. I must not get stressed about this.

The weather can unglue the yearly goals, too. This year we planned to make 300 tonnes of silage so we could feed calves and yearlings through the winter. The spring was dry, we made 90 tonnes. Maybe we cannot keep the calves as planned. But we will have to keep all the lambs, unplanned, because there is no market for lambs on account of the dairy boom and the drought.

Meanwhile, in the city, there are skyscrapers full of goal-setters spending hours and hours, being paid good money, to set goals which probably do not alter behaviours very much at all. Look at New Year's resolutions. They are goals — and how long does it take before the resolution to perform better begins to wear off? A month? Significant others point this out, but the person gets very angry.

You will be missed, Janice, I imagine creative writers are sought-after people in the goal-writing business.

Dear Virginia

Margaret has newly-sprouted green energy, like the pushing pumpkin vine in my garden which is growing out of its wire-netting cage because we're having so much rain. She looked out of her office window at all the grey rain. 'You know,' she said, 'we should plant the raised bed with lettuce.' We all looked. She was right.

Although our offices are three storeys off the ground, the

third storey is smaller than the second and is girdled around with a tiled flat area where pigeons and gulls congregate for meetings. No one suns themselves on this terrace. That's not what one does at work. No one even goes out there for a smoke now. With the new legislation, the terrace is off-limits for smoking. On this deserted tiled wasteland are tiled raised beds. A few have agapanthus in them. They're flowering nicely because of all the summer rain. Most have belladonna — deadly nightshade — in them, and nothing else. One of the tiled raised beds is exactly outside Margaret's office window. It is, hence, referred to as 'our' raised bed by Margaret and her pod-mates Raewyn and Kiri.

After a project report, and some contracts written, I heard squeaky whispers outside my door. Margaret and Raewyn trooped into my room after peering around the door to make sure I wasn't 'with' anyone (ie, having a meeting). 'Yes,' I agreed, 'I will go home at lunchtime and get trowels.' I looked out of my own window. Unfortunately I don't have a raised bed outside mine. Margaret and I went down in the lift together; she to buy seedling lettuces and silverbeet at the garden centre under the supermarket, and I to get the trowels. That afternoon Margaret and Raewyn toiled like peasants.

Next morning, when I arrived at work, the trowels were in two plastic bags, an inner and an outer bag, on my office computer chair. Putting anything on someone's chair is the very best way to guarantee they will see it. Never put important items in a person's in-tray where it will form part of the office compost. I rushed into Margaret's office and looked outside. The raised bed had neat rows of lettuces and silverbeet, and behind them a sheltering tangle of belladonna.

Dear Janice

I had a very bad hiccup on my first shearing morning. I mixed the waffle mixture and poured the first waffle into the iron, when *POP!* went the fuse and a little puff of acrid electrical smoke spurted from the iron, and it died.

Thank goodness a waffle mixture is easily transmogrified into pikelets — which is what I made with the batter — but I knew the shearers, and particularly the shed hands, would be disappointed. Waffles are my signature turn for morning tea. The shed hands always ask Harry, 'Will there be waffles today?' There are not always waffles. Sometimes I do ginger gems from the Edmonds cook-book. I have two very old gem irons made from heavy iron and they make beautiful gems, another old-fashioned little morning-tea item and a precursor to muffins, I think.

Here is the waffle recipe. I do not know where it came from originally, but I have had it since I was ten, when, as a special treat, Dorothy Clark, Mother's best friend, lent us her waffle iron. The Clarks were the only family in Manutuke who travelled overseas in the 'fifties. Somewhere on her travels, maybe it was at Harrod's, Dorothy bought a waffle iron. It was the first waffle iron we had ever seen, and after the Clarks tired of waffles we were allowed to borrow it.

I had read about waffles in *What Katie Did At School*, where Katie and Clover always had waffles with maple syrup as a last meal before entering the prison that was boarding school. You couldn't buy maple syrup in New Zealand in the 'fifties. It was a prohibited luxury under the strict import licensing regime, so we made do with golden syrup. I still love waffles and golden syrup, and so do the shearers.

Waffles

1 cup flour
2 tsp baking powder
¼ tsp salt
1 tbsp sugar
2 large eggs
¾ cup milk
2 tbsp melted butter

Turn on the waffle iron — it takes a while to heat.

Into a bowl sift the flour, baking powder and salt. Separate the eggs and beat the whites until stiff. Beat the yolks with the sugar until thick and creamy.

Mix the milk and egg-yolk mixture together, and stir into the dry ingredients along with the melted butter. Lastly add the beaten egg whites, fold in gently to retain the air.

My waffle iron is the same as Mrs Clark's waffle iron. It's one of the old-fashioned ones that isn't a throwaway made of Teflon-coated metal and plastic. It is a very good, metal iron. Harry repaired it for me and so it lives again to make many more waffles for the shearers. The recipe does make very excellent pikelets as well.

Dear Virginia

Success! Your strawberry conserve recipe has worked. Diana from The Catlins was here recently and she's been eating it straight out of the fridge.

Dear Janice

This is siesta time. The idea of pre-dawn starts is that there is siesta time, as in lying back for an hour and reading a book, but this goal is not adhered to. Harry is out repairing troughs and water leaks, Hamish is spraying gorse, and I'm writing whilst baking the week's bread and waiting for the blackcurrant sorbet syrup to cool.

Sorbets are very easy to make if you have an ice-cream machine.

Blackcurrant Sorbet
500g blackcurrants
½ cup water
1¼ cups water
½ cup caster sugar
2 tbsp cassis (nice but not necessary)
2 egg whites

Turn the blackcurrants into juice by boiling in ½ cup of water until pulpy and then straining. Put 1¼ cups water and the sugar into a pot, stir over a low heat until the sugar is dissolved. Bring to the boil and boil rapidly for 10 minutes. Cool the syrup.

When the blackcurrant juice and the sugar syrup are cold, combine them. I don't add all the blackcurrant juice at once as it is very strong; I like to add to taste. Fold in the beaten egg whites. I have the ice-cream machine running and I pour the sorbet mixture in through the spout. My machine takes about 10 minutes to freeze the mixture. It is delicious, tart and tangy. A little goes a long way.

You can make sorbets out of any kind of fruit. I make raspberry, blackcurrant and orange sorbets. Kate, a chef friend, makes a delicious feijoa one.

I find it hard to write precise recipes — I just noticed 'precise' is an anagram of 'recipes' — as I'm always making things by taste and feel.

I have to go now. Writing was not part of the daily goal; I will now return to earlier set goal of mowing the drive and the grass around Kit's pond.

PS: All the vegetables and berries at this time of the year are grown in the garden. It is a sweet moment when you can look at a meal and know that all the food has travelled less than a mile!!!! No carbon hoofprint here.

Dear Virginia

That isn't siesta time! You were doing three different things at once, and you called it siesta time! You put harassed project managers to shame. If you were here, you'd be shunned for being over-efficient.

There is no carbon, copy or footprint, of any sort here either; the greening of the office continues. Phillipa and Christine are running a plant-rescue service where editors and designers with low horticultural skills can call on them for re-potting, or restructuring. So look out. If they start moving you into a bigger room or pulling your arms off, you'll know you've been vegetating and are about to be restructured.

Cathy stole Vina's pot plant. Vina demanded it back. Cathy sent a ransom email — coffees every morning from the Fuel cart. She disguised the plant with sunglasses. This is the sort of bizarre behaviour that happens in offices and never in outdoor jobs. Rupert takes cuttings from the expensive Rent-o-Kill plants around the office, puts them in water. When they root, he pots them up in coffee cups on the windowsill. He intends selling them to team-mates. His triffid-like begonia was an innocent cutting from Judy eighteen months ago. Since then, the plant has revealed its ambition to take over more of the pod than one worker is allowed. Hacking it back with his office scissors is on his daily To Do schedule in Meeting Maker. The cause of the current accommodation crisis and the need for a complete re-fit of the pods on Level Four is probably due to the plant.

The lines between work and home are blurring. No more late evenings with the bag of licorice. I leave in two weeks.

Hello, Janice

Last week we had four Danes to visit. We often have Danish visitors, a legacy from Rikke who arrived at Double Tops for a week in December in 1987. She stayed with us for four months.

Danes like salads. Every Danish visitor we have ever entertained has been passionate about salad. In a brave move I decided to forget the salad thing and cook the traditional lamb roast.

Lambs home-killed are the lucky ones. If you have to die it is easier and less frightening to die at home. Because they are shot unawares, the meat is very tender. Do I have to tell you this? Yes, everyone who eats meat has to be reminded that animals have to die and that they are killed as gently as possible.

The Danes said they liked our well-cooked lamb roast and the potatoes with mint and the carrots, but after podding the peas I think they thought the peas should have been served raw to provide that little dash of salad.

I grew Kinbi carrots (King's Seeds) this spring, and every-body, absolutely every single person who has eaten a Kinbi, has asked, 'What *are* these carrots?' They are pale gold, and soft when cooked, and they evoke memories of a summer childhood so they must be old-fashioned carrots. The only drawback with the Kinbi is that half the plants run to seed and do not produce a root. My friend Rodney, who once worked on seed research, told me that heritage vegetables do have a tendency to go to seed; this is a natural inbuilt survival trait. Modern seeds have been selectively bred to not run to seed early.

Kinbi Carrots with Parsley

Cook the carrots in salted water until barely soft, drain and add a little butter, chopped parsley and lots of ground black pepper. Swish around in the saucepan and pour out onto a serving dish.

Next morning the sun was hot and dry, a nor'wester was roaring in the trees. I took the Danes driving up over the Milo top track to the Pathos gates, the lonely windy crossroads between Phipps, Milo and Mjolfjel, where the view to all four points of the compass offers no sign of another living creature — apart from sheep and the odd wheeling hawk. They were unusually subdued on the drive up — the track is narrow with a steep drop into a gully, and maybe being driven by a woman is not the expected thing. The senior detective from Copenhagen was gripping the panic bar in the passenger front seat, out of panic or for stability I did not know.

When we returned, we dragged a table and chairs into the shade of the laburnum tree and spread out a shared feast. 'You won't like our food,' declared Lotte. After all the cooked vegetables the night before, I suppose they expected, well, more cooked vegetables. We laid out our standard lunch and they laid out theirs, and they were identical — almost.

Danes cannot live without salad and they cannot live without rye bread. They had rye pumpernickel. We had Molenberg. And we both had cheese, salami, lettuce, tomatoes, cucumber and salmon. The difference: they had chopped onions and a large bulb of garlic. They made sandwiches with thick-sliced garlic and tomato. Not wanting to appear timorous about so large a slug of garlic, we made ourselves garlic sandwiches on pumpernickel, too. Try it, it is yum and you cannot smell yourself at all.

When the Danes left they presented us with a bottle of Gammel Dansk bitters. They said, 'It is good for you, good to drink at any time of the night or day.' The label says that the exquisite soft and dry flavour derives from a blend of twenty-nine different herbs and fruits. When they said 'it is good for you', they were correct. It is extremely medicinal, very bitter and very absolutely an acquired taste. If you know any Danes who are pining for a bottle of Gammel Dansk as New

Zealanders pine for Marmite, let me know. I cannot swallow it without gagging.

How's the roof-top garden project going?

Dear Virginia

After the planting of Margaret's raised bed, the word has spread. People from the other side of the building where there are no raised beds have flocked into Margaret's office to see the new, and vaguely subversive, garden. Someone covered for the receptionist so she could slip away from the phones for a few minutes. Maxine suggested they pull out all the belladonna. Diana advised putting mizuma into the bed. 'Who's Miss Zuma?' asked Simon. Mikala wanted radishes. Someone else thought nasturtiums would look lovely.

'They'd trail,' she said wistfully. 'And we could eat the leaves in our lunch salads.'

The greening of the office has begun. And I can now leave it in good hands. And they are all my friends, and I will miss working with them.

February

Dear Virginia

I think I'm in shock. I'm trying to be unemployed, to live in the moment, enjoying what is around me rather than what is on my To Do list and spreadsheets. This doesn't come naturally, but it is easier if I try this out in the beloved garden. My garden is, at the moment, a jungle in which Stanley could not guarantee to find Livingstone. It's all about 6–7 feet high. The sweet peas are now brown and yellow and sere. There is oxalis everywhere. The catmint is so tall you can't walk past it along the path. I wander, sipping perc'd coffee — so much better than plunged. And I smell all the plants around me: star jasmine, Christmas lilies, *Nicotiana sylvestris*, tomato leaves, sage, basil, and the last of the sweet peas. I pull out spent plants; if the pods of the sweet peas rattle, I put my hand around them carefully so that when they burst in my palm I don't lose the precious seed of this very colourful, very fragrant variety. Fine poppy seed puffs out the top of its globular pod. I watch the fantails flitter, and hear the blackbirds. Behind the birds is the hum of the motorway, from here one uninterrupted soughing sound, like surf.

Back in the kitchen, I lean against the blue kitchen bench and read Billy Collins. What a treat: to read a Billy Collins poem rather than an action plan! And reading a poem in the middle of the morning! I read 'You, Reader' from his *The Trouble with Poetry* collection. The poem is about him witting at his table, beside a bowl of pears. He describes the reader, his reader, who wants to be a writer:

you, leaning in a doorway somewhere,
near some blue hydrangeas, reading this.

I look up and there, in full bosomy bloom, under the red-satin Dublin Bay roses, are the blue hydrangeas.

Point taken, Billy. I'm leaning. So I'm not writing. But that's fine. It's summertime. And suddenly there is no hurry.

This is just to say I am here, disorganized, and hanging by a thread, but I will let you know what happens to your normally frantic friend as leisure rolls out before her, like a red carpet.

Dear Janice

Leisure, there's no time for leisure here, wash your mouth out. It's Coast to Coast time again. Although we've been writing for a long time, I've never written about this mad race. Mad because, when you think about it, it's a mad idea — running, kayaking and cycling from Kumara beach on the west coast of the South Island to Sumner beach on the east coast. A 243-kilometre journey all in one day, a journey that Arthur Dudley Dobson the explorer took months to complete.

Fleur began her C-to-C career as the running half of a team that came second-last; her kayaking partner stopped, *in extremis*, to smoke a cigarette on the river bank. Two years ago she won The Longest Day — the one-day race. Last year, defending her title, she lost it by forty-two seconds; heart-breaking for us, her support crew, because it's easy to imagine where you might have made or lost forty-two seconds in transitions.

Transitions are like clothing relay races, those ones we raced as children where you had to put on a set of clothes, run to the other end, take them off and give them to the next competitor. Remember the 'all fingers and thumbs' feeling? The secret of the transition is not to panic.

Transitions are fuel stops as well as gear changes. Support crews have a detailed food and water plan, and plastic boxes for each transition with lots of labelled packets and bottles. There is food to stuff into shorts and shirt pockets, food to stick on the kayak paddle, there are water bottles for the bike, water bottles for transition, energy drinks, bladders of sports drink for the kayak. Fleur's food is a little more complex than most; she is a celiac, so everything must be gluten-free. 'Food' is a euphemism, 'sustenance' would be a better word; it's mostly disgusting, particularly the leppin. Sounds like a leprous lemon? It is. A leppin is a squeezy tube of energy gel that makes you want to throw up at the same time you're trying to swallow it.

I want to tell you what it is like to be a support person. It is the same routine every year — just different results.

Coast to Coast 2009

Hokitika. At 3am it's dark; a warm wind blows, but there is no rain. The lights in the motels across the way are on; in each motel the support crews are creeping about, making breakfast, checking the transition boxes, making last-minute adjustments. We wake our athlete at four. I feed her gluten-free pancakes and maple syrup, gluten-free toast and a cup of decaffeinated coffee which she doesn't drink. She is silent, so are we; it seems best. At a quarter to five the athletes begin driving out; we are last to leave, old hands. We play the Feelers' 'Beautiful Day' very loud, over and over all the way to Kumara.

Kumara junction at 5am. The road is like a glow-worm

cave, the dark twinkles with bobbing lights, headlamp torches, winking cycle lights at front and tail. We find bike rack No. 144 and hang Fleur's bike on the wire, she wraps herself in a survival blanket, we hug her, wish her luck and join the convoy to Aitkens. A wind blows strong against the car and the dawn sneaks up on the night, turning the mountains into dark turrets against the pale morning sky.

Aitkens at 6am. We shiver, waiting two hours in the freezing morning for the first cycle bunch. A coal train grinds past, long, black and sinister with its covered wagons and groaning iron wheels. We wait, and then we hear the helicopter which presages the arrival of the first cyclists. The cycle transition at Aitkens is a tidal wave, cyclists rushing in, pushing, shoving, bikes are flung down and support crews thrust forwards trying to find their cyclists — panic and pandemonium. Helmet off, ankle straps off, pack on, dried bananas slapped into a hand and she's gone. Silence. The successful support crews trek back to their cars, the rest wait on.

Klondyke Corner, waiting at the bush edge of the Mingha river, the two-day circus crowd has moved on, a lone coffee cart is doing a slow trade, and the local school breakfast tent is shutting up shop. I sit on an official chair in the sun waiting for Fleur to run up the grassy chute. There is a long time between runners after the leading men have pounded through. We hear a cheering that heralds someone special and know it will be the first woman, but who? I recognize Fleur's gait and leap to my feet. We run together as I pass her the bike helmet, a drink bottle, a rolled pancake, Dinah holds the bike, I stuff leppins into Fleur's shirt pocket and she's off on the 15k bike ride to the Mount White transition. We rush to the car so we can arrive at transition before her. I wait at the top of the Mount White road, waiting to grab the bike and pass Fleur a handful of GF sandwiches to munch as she lopes down to her kayak at the river.

The Waimakariri River at the gorge bridge is the last transition. The day is almost done and so are the competitors. I sit on the grass at the bike racks and watch weary 'two-day' racers who are racing to say that they have taken part in the race from one side of the South Island to the other. The race has been won hours earlier; there is no urgency in their transitions, they sit on folding chairs to change their shoes, and they chat and munch food before they push off for the bike ride to Sumner. The tempo lifts as the first 'one-day' men streak up the hill with their entourages, flinging off clothes as they run, drinking and eating as they're managed through their shoe change and pushed off on their bicycles. The first woman runs in from the river; it is not Fleur.

Sumner. The crowds have gone by the time the first 'one-day' woman support crews arrive at the finish line; the sun is sinking low in the sky and families are packing up their children after a day at the beach. The press loiters to take last photos of the day, and cold loyal supporters line the chute and wait.

Two years ago it was Fleur who breasted the Speight's Ale tape; we were swamped with news-hounds and photographers and radio hosts. Last year Fleur was besieged again: how did it feel to be a forty-two-seconds loser? This year, after being picked to win and suffering a series of mechanical misfortunes, Fleur ran fourth, the press had gone home, the wind was freezing, we were yesterday's news.

Dear Virginia

Ohmygawd! What can I say? Go, Fleur, for your next big race, you amazing woman.

Now, back to the food . . . I guess a leppin is what you eat when food is simply physical sustenance. It's like being on a drip in hospital. While you have all been rising at dawn and exerting yourselves, I've been reading about the other end of the food continuum from leppins, the *haute cuisine* end, and in particular about a chef from the molecular-gastronomy movement. He serves edible strings of corn silk on herb stems; or a sphere with a strawberry centre, then a layer of *niçoise* olives, and a crust of white chocolate flavoured with violets. Or dehydrated bacon wrapped in apple leather. Or how about smouldering oak leaves surrounding a poached pheasant? Or, the best one of all, in a restaurant that doesn't believe in using ovens — a hot ramekin of orange peel, nutmeg, allspice, sage and goose fat — to remind diners of the smell of opening the oven door on Christmas Day, a smell all those diners haven't smelt since childhood.

In case you are wanting the recipe for the strawberry/olive/violet ball — the chef dipped a strawberry in the olive mixture then flash-froze them in liquid nitrogen before wrapping the chocolate around the whole thing.

Our taste buds can tell sweet, salty, bitter and sour, but they can't tell beef from lamb. We need our nose and eyes for that. It's interesting that you have to put the whole sensory picture together to make taste. You know that thing about some apples being like onions if you eat them with a blindfold on and a peg over your nose. (Not a required activity if you come and dine with me.) The flavour of something is all about the memory of that taste. This means it's important what we feed our children.

We can actually train them to like healthy food. People who cannot taste aren't motivated to eat, so taste is essential for survival.

On the continuum of food from leppins to extreme *haute cuisine*, I guess I'm in the middle — I'm happy with simple food to nourish us, body and soul. And as I'm not about to train for a Coast to Coast, I hope I never have to swallow a leppin.

Dear Janice

After months of dry days the tussock is tinder-dry. The 11th of February was such a day, the hot wind screaming off the mountains. And then it stilled, a storm rolled in from all around with thunder and lightning and torrential rain. The rain fell in curtains, pelting the roof and bouncing off the hard, dry lawn. Sometime after dark the phone rang. Heather from Haydon Downs, suppressed panic in her voice, said the shed behind the house was alight. She had rung the fire brigade, but could Harry come and help. I stayed at home and rang the rest of the neighbours. Harry raced up the road. The rain kept falling.

Harry arrived home after midnight. 'Haydon Downs is buggered,' he said. He stank of smoke, but he crawled into bed anyway. 'The water pressure was useless,' he said. It was a mere trickle crawling from the hose, but the rain was bucketing down so he wrenched the downpipe from the guttering, and he and Mark and Barry formed a bucket relay. More neighbours arrived. They managed to slow the progress of the flames, which began crackling under the eaves of the house as the fire brigade arrived. The firefighters punched holes into the kitchen ceiling and hosed the flames which had exploded into the roof space. Water seeped through the ceiling and soaked the carpets. The kitchen was stained with smoke, and the lights were doused.

Heather and Barry stayed the night at Melrose. The tussock telegraph cranked into operation at dawn. By lunchtime, four houses for temporary accommodation had been offered, food arrived on the doorstep, friends and neighbours rallied around to help with the clean-up. I made two 'emergency pizzas', but when I met Heather on the road and told her I'd bring them up she said they had 'food for Africa' and please to keep them for something else, so I put them in the deep-freeze for an emergency of our own.

Emergency Pizza is the name for a pizza that can be made in five minutes. It is a life-saver when you have an unexpected need for a very quick meal. There are a few pantry essentials required for emergency pizza. Country cooks need pantry essentials, because we cannot pop down to the supermarket or drop by the deli on the way home from work. Pantry essentials for emergency pizza are: pizza bases in the deep-freeze, a jar of flavoured tomato mix, olives, onions, bacon or salami, cheese, oregano (fresh is best).

I like home-made pizza bases best, but I don't always have them. I keep pita bread in the deep-freeze. It makes a firm and chewy base. I use Edam cheese. Mozzarella is expensive and I would only use it for a special designer pizza with expensive and exotic toppings.

Dear Virginia

I make pizzas for emergencies, too; my emergencies are sudden invasions of nephews, or too many people arriving for FEDs. I use Purebake organic pizza bases if I don't make my own. They are wonderfully crisp. Sliced home-grown tomatoes and chopped onion and bacon and a little cheese, with lots of dried thyme — better flavour than fresh. Perfect. The crust is hard. The tomatoes are so soft and so sweet. And just to see the pizza coming out of the oven, bubbling and smelling wonderful. I have to fight people away from it; never cut it until it's sat for 10 minutes.

Instead of fire, I will write to you of water. When the heat rises in Wellington, there is nothing for it but to throw in the trowel, phone Jane, and head for Shelley Bay. My friendship with Jane celebrates two shared delights: walking and swimming. We have been walking and/or swimming on Sunday afternoons for twenty-three years, thirteen of them with Bunsen. We have been on more than a thousand walks together. Wellington's walking tracks are our slowed-down version of the Coast to Coast. We don't take leppins, or a support crew, but we do do picnics and thermoses. Today's swim and picnic had all the right bit-players: there were Global Challenge yachts with beige sails setting off on the next leg of their absurdly expensive and unnecessary 'personal challenge'. (Why don't they just get a job teaching if they want to change their lives in a challenging way?) The big yachts were buzzed by helicopters. Little P Class boats, much bigger challenges for most people, fluttered like butterflies in Lyall Bay. The tug trolloped past, in red, and smoking.

Jellyfish congregated for a Big Blob Out, and a wimpish man (on a short, chaperoned escape from the computer, I suspect) told me not to go in. I took my jellyfish sweeper — a piece of wood — into the water with me to clear a path through them. They were at the edge of the sea only, like lace at the hem of a skirt.

The water was exhilarating. It swirled around in many different folds, some warm, some very cold. It took a while before I put my head under, but when I did I saw the pale legs of the computer man's dog stretching out, running in the sea. I threw the jellyfish-sweeper stick as far out as I could, and dog and I raced, our necks stretched as long as Nefertiti's. He grabbed the stick — in his teeth, of course — and I reared backward quickly so that when he turned suddenly I wouldn't get the stick in my eye.

We were out there, on the huge lit-up stage that is the harbour. All around us was land. You couldn't tell there was a passage out to the heads. A ferry went past. It seemed to slide into the wings.

The dog reached the shore with his stick. He turned and faced us, sitting in the water, smiling. We floated back in and attended to the serious business of the picnic: huge slabs of ham, soft bap rolls, tomatoes from my garden, Kapiti *brie*. And almond fingers for dessert. They have *Made in Holland* on the wrapper, AND *Made in Mangere*. I imagined the world's largest Polynesian city, in Holland, full of ice-skating Samoans.

Then we threw ourselves into the sea for that essential second swim. The jellyfish bobbed in rows. Maybe they have each fought for a front-row seat at the very edge of their known universe, from where they watch the equally jelly-like but very clumsy humans. It's a thought.

PS: How are Barry and Heather?

Hello, Janice

Barry and Heather are very well, they are survivors. They're living in the Haydon Downs granny cottage for the meantime, power, telephone and Sky connected, and they have an old wringer washing machine outside under the eaves. The homestead is to be restored.

The downpour yielded 150ml of rain and the drought was over. If the shed had caught fire earlier in the day when the wind was blowing and the temperatures were in the mid-thirties, Haydon Downs and all our houses to the east of it would have burned and there would have been charred sheep littering the hills. We felt lucky.

We have guests from Zambia staying tonight — British, not indigenous, Zambians. When Liz wants something done in the garden she instructs the gardener and it is done, and she has a maid and two night-guards and all her tomatoes grow. Should I go to Zambia, I wonder?

Dear Virginia

No. Not if you don't like drought. Stay here and make cheese, bread, ice cream and waffles. Roast a lamb. Admire your glass-house. I can't imagine you sitting back watching other people do those things for you. Enjoy the summer.

Summer food is easy food. It is the month of avocados. In

the supermarket now there are bags of Hass avos for $2. That's about 40¢ an avo. An easy lunch.

Avocado Spread

Cut two avocados in half and remove the stones by squeezing the avo gently. In a bowl, squeeze half a lemon onto the avocado pulp. To get a juicy lemon: roll it up and down the bench. Leave it in the sun. Do this until the lemon is softened. Then, when you cut it, it will be full of juice.

So, add the juice to the avocado, with a little olive oil, and mash with a fork. Add a pinch of salt — none for Harry, though — pepper or some chopped chilli (which looks wonderful, the red flecks in the green). And pile onto toast. That's a big mound of it on a round of toast. Don't add garlic. Too harsh. Let the avo flavour and texture speak. That has to be the easiest summer lunch.

Another meal I make at summer's end is *minestrone*.

Minestrone

I sweat some chopped onion in olive oil, with garlic and any herbs in the garden that look as though they are crying out for a haircut — so thyme and coriander and oregano are the most common ones I use for this. Add salt. (Or not.)

Then I pile into the pot all the tomatoes I've picked from the sagging, exhausted plants. If your tomatoes are big ones — like Oxheart and Beefsteak — you could plunge them into a pot of boiling water for a few minutes then spoon them out and leave them to cool first. That way you can just roll the skins off them — like pantyhose after a long day at work. If I find any ancient beans, about a foot long, with leathery skins, totally unsuitable for eating, I shuck the big pink and black seeds out of these and add the seeds to the pot. I add any other vegetable I have too much of in the garden — the odd carrot, some spinach, etc. And I simmer the whole lot for half an hour.

Then I wait until it's cool, transfer it to those bottles and jars that always self-replicate under the sink. Simple.

Radha has the skill of gift-giving. She gave me a potted black-pepper plant. Ornamental, I thought. But no: it produced peppers all through the summer. The special thing here is that the peppers are small and black — very attractive not just *in* containers but *as* containers. So they will be stuffed with a very rich mixture of lentils and tomatoes — all the tomatoes are from the garden. I picked coriander seeds, ground them up — see, I now have the time — sautéed them with chopped onions, then added garlic and all the other things. This will be packed into the peppers tomorrow and baked for family dinner.

We will also have a green salad (garden) and fish, unfortunately from a fish shop because Robert is not living at home or working on a fishing boat any more. (There was that one wonderful day when I was plodding home along Tinakori Road and he biked up, with one hand on the handlebars and one holding up high a platter with a large crayfish on it. 'For your tea,' he said.)

And talking of Robert: he's coming home, that is to Auckland. He's returning with his Irish girlfriend, Mia, to a job as a rescue helicopter pilot. Rowan, my much-loved sister-in-law, is having a big birthday soon and we will all be together, even a brother-in-law from England. And I will have time to cook!

Dear Janice

How clever of you to grow black peppers. I suppose they have been propagated especially for the Wellington executive garden.

We have a plague of hares. It is not unusual to see thirty hares in one paddock. They're mad creatures, hippity-hopping and dancing in pairs, but they eat a lot so must be curtailed. In wintertime when it is possible to hang a hare for the required week in the cold, I'm going to keep a few carcasses and make jugged hare — without the fresh blood, because it sounds disgusting. I shall use Constance Spry and of course I shall look up the mad Alice B Toklas book in case she cooked jugged hare for Gertrude or some other famous writer or painter.

Driven inside by cold rain. Winter approaches. Sinking into a black funk at the thought of seven months of winter woollies.

Dear Virginia

I can't imagine looking out the kitchen window and sizing up the wildlife for the cooking pot. The postie? The chunky courier driver? The meter reader? The squeezer?* I will need a whole lot of new recipes to meet that challenge.

* See *Common Ground*.

I'm still organizing my study, after leaving work four weeks ago. I haven't tidied up the files I dumped on the floor in the last week of work. I don't know yet how to spend my time or earn my living. But I must move on. Just for a while I will drift like kelp with the tide. I am practising slowing down.

You described farming in *Common Ground* as being like a game of Monopoly, each year a circuit. Cooking seems to me a daily circuit of preparing, cooking, eating, and cleaning up. Gardening is an annual circuit. They both make me aware that we get to do the circuits many times, but that, for us, they are finite. Because I know I can't cook and garden forever, I treasure those times in the kitchen and garden. Because I'm so aware of life's impermanence, I enjoy what for some could be seen as chores. I like to sieve tiny grains of life through a sieve. Nature, however, cycles forever and hence never needs to linger to appreciate itself.

> Nature's cyclical return
> versus man's blind rush to the grave.

wrote Billy Collins in 'Themes'.

I live an absurdly busy life — writing, tutoring, directing audio productions — so gardening and cooking are essential because they slow the world down for me. Meet the new, slow me. I garden carefully and slowly. I cook slowly. I never put a pot on to boil and go out of the kitchen. That's when I stand, looking out the window at the garden and the birds. I enjoy chopping, peeling, scrubbing. I clean up after myself as I cook. My cooking is all neat and tidy and organized. I take time to enjoy the gradation of colour in ripening tomatoes, from lime green to bright red. I love the different reds of all the heritage tomatoes I grow.

I go out a lot, but coming home is always good. The first thing I do when I get home is put on the kettle. I walk around the garden sipping tea, thinking about what I will cook that night and enjoying the garden. I know I've written to you about dining out, whiling away hours in cafés. But that is my way of contrasting my life with yours, particularly my now-departed office life.

I love returning home best of all. With dirt-stained hands, I enjoy working hard in the garden, a peasant hiding in the CBD. I always prefer having people over for dinner than going to a restaurant. I am someone who likes to be at home. It is sometimes as hard to get me out of the house as it is to get a walnut out of its shell.

I'd like to leave you with a more accurate picture of the real me. Today the sun is shining and the cicadas are singing. I've been helping someone write a novel this morning. At lunchtime I go into the garden and pick one sweet new zucchini, two tomatoes, lots of beans and some chives and thyme. This is all within ten steps of the back door.

In the kitchen I heat the black cast-iron pan, swirl in oil, add garlic, then add lots of coriander seeds. I keep a bouquet of dried coriander plants in a jar. They look beautiful, a golden tangle with tiny shiny round jewels scattered throughout. I listen to the seeds popping and scattering in the pan. Then I top and tail the beans and strip off the stringy sides as they are getting a bit elderly. I put the lid on and cook them slowly with the zucchini, tomatoes and chives. While they are cooking I walk down the drive and check the mail shed. I read my mail surrounded by the smell of my *ratatouille*. Then I tip it into a wide bowl in which I've cut cubes of feta. That's the only thing in the lunch that I didn't grow.

Ratatouille isn't something you cook from a recipe book.

Like *minestrone*, it's a dish designed to be flexible. It's all about using whatever the garden will provide.

We sit under the plum tree in the shade and eat, and talk about the newly formed residents' association. Then I let two children who have arrived pick two red apples from the tree for their after-school treat.

Dear Janice

A month without the regular direct-credit salary landing in your account each fortnight and still coffee-ing and lunching as if it were. You will be starting to get a feel for the great worry of the self-employed. How is the bank balance looking this week? Do I need to speak to my bank manager about an 'accommodation'? You will have to get used to the 'time is money' maxim. Any time you are not working, you are not earning. Loitering over long business lunches is no longer paid for. But, you will love the freedom of being your own employer. 'I will work Saturday and Sunday and I can take Tuesday and Wednesday off.' It is a wonderful freedom.

One day I would like to 'move on' as you have done. I would like to live beside the sea in my own house. You may think that an odd thing to say, but I live in my mother-in-law's house. Mandy and I often talk of feeling like interlopers in the houses our husbands grew up in. Somehow, though never spoken of, 'Mother' is still there. I do not think moving is an option any time soon. One lovely summer's afternoon in January I overheard Harry telling a visiting Swedish timber merchant that he planned to die here. Harry is looking extremely healthy since his ankles became thin again, so I do not think death is imminent. I dream of the sound of waves crashing on a beach. Sometimes I wish that sombre owl and the kidney shutdown had given Harry a sense of vulnerability, but neither has dissuaded him from farming on into the setting sun. The love of ancestral land is strong. So we'll throw a six to start, and play another year until we pass Go again.

I know I said we were imprisoned by the seasons, circuiting the Monopoly board, passing Go once a year, but there are places to get off and loiter for a while. So I'll be happy on the circuit, and happy with my house full of ghosts. That is what happens when you live in the same house for a very long time. When we sit down to Christmas or Easter lunches, at shearing and at dinner parties, there are chairs that once were sat upon by some other guest. Some of the diners have gone forever, and others have moved on to somewhere else. It is fun to look back. None of the memories is unhappy. It is best to discard the sad ones, though maybe they are never really discarded. I once read a poem which went something like this:

> Time doesn't heal
> the memories.
> It merely buries them
> in shallow graves.

Index of recipes